THE DELPHIN GARDEn

C000004727

A COMPREHENSIVE GUIDE TO GROWING DELPHINIUMS

This book is dedicated to the memory of Richard Wainwright, who was the President of The Delphinium Society for many years. Also to the memory of many good Delphinium Society friends who include Roy Latty, Stuart Ogg, George Radley, Dora Larkan and Terry Murphy.

Published 2003 ~ By The Delphinium Society

Editor ~ Patrick Booth
Editorial Consultant ~ Les Cooper

Writing team: David Bassett, Shirley Bassett, Anne Blissett, Patrick Booth, Allan Cook Les Cooper, Duncan McGlashan, Ray Joslyn, Nigel Moody, Kees Sahin and John Thirkell

Illustrations by: David Bassett, Patrick Booth, Duncan Hagan, John Flowerday and Nigel Moody

The Delphinium Society is a registered Charity ~ No 259202

Printed by Headley Bros Ltd., The Invicta Press, Queens Road., Ashford, Kent TN24 8HH

ISBN 0-9543877-0-8

CONTENTS

FOREWORD

The Delphinium Society was established in 1928 and has, as its objectives, the popularisation of growing, breeding and exhibiting delphiniums. We believe that this new publication is an appropriate way to mark its 75th anniversary, satisfying a need for comprehensive and up to date information about our favourite flowers. We hope you enjoy the book and find it useful. It was conceived as a co-operative endeavour, with individual chapters being contributed by our general committee members. As such, it reads very much like an anthology with some personal opinions being expressed and certainly with a variety of writing styles. My task, as Editor, has been fascinating. Despite growing delphiniums for over 30 years, I have learned an awful lot about them that I didn't know before. The book could not have been produced without the willing help of Les Cooper, who has acted as Editorial Consultant. Other Delphinium Society members, as well as members of the staff at the R.H.S. garden at Wisley, have also given a great deal of help, for which I thank them.

It is just over 150 years since the creation of the first garden delphiniums in the form that we think of them now. They have been improved constantly and are now the crowning glory of mid summer flower displays. They are reliable and tough hardy perennial plants that can be grown in any country having a temperate climate. They are very frost resistant and can be grown even in countries with extremely cold winters such as Canada and Iceland. If care and attention is given, and good cultivars or seedlings are grown, the results should be spectacular and deeply satisfying.

This book is a celebration of the delphinium in all its variety. It gives advice on exhibiting, breeding and hybridising. There is guidance about growing some species and annual seed strains, as well as descriptions of them. Chapters on cultivation are written, mainly, for the benefit of those who wish to grow the elatum hybrids. The advice is applicable, also, to the more dainty 'Belladonna' and 'Connecticut Yankee' hybrids, which have a bushy style of growth and provide repeat flowering during the summer months.

Delphiniums are wonderful plants. Contrary to what many gardeners think, they are quite easy to grow although extra time and trouble is needed to deal with slugs and snails, and to stake the plants. The results, however, are very rewarding. There are no better plants for many situations in the garden. The tall growing elatum hybrids are essential for the backs of flower borders, with a wonderful colour range that extends through every variation of blue, to purples, mauves, creams, whites and magenta pinks. There are shorter growing elatum hybrids for smaller gardens as well as a number of garden worthy species.

CHAPTER ONE

HISTORICAL OUTLINE

By Patrick Booth

Mention delphiniums to most gardeners and they will immediately picture the highly developed garden hybrids that feature in flower borders during June and July. However, the history of the modern hybrids goes back to the species from which those sophisticated beauties have been developed.

Delphiniums are so named because the ancient Greeks and Romans thought that the unopened flower buds of the species *Delphinium peregrinum* resembled miniature dolphins. The earliest references to them are in the writings of Pliny the Elder in his 'Naturale Historia' and of Pedanios Dioscorides, a greek physician in the Roman army during the first century A.D., who produced 'De Materia Medica', containing over 400 colour illustrations, descriptions and suggested uses of plants. Those early writers noted the extremely poisonous nature of *D. staphisagria*, which has been used to control head lice on humans and, in very small doses, as an emetic and purgative.

Whilst the decorative appearance of plants has always been recognised, their use solely for garden display is a relatively modern innovation. They were valued in past times mostly for their useful, rather than aesthetic, qualities. Thus the yellow flowered species *D. zalil*, now reclassified by botanists as a form of *D. semibarbatum*, is still used for dyeing silk in Iraq, Iran and Afghanistan. In America, the Kiowa tribe of Indians used the seeds of *D. carolinianum*, the prairie larkspur, in their ceremonial rattles. In Italy, no doubt, seeds of *D. staphisagria* found their way into the darker recesses of the Borgia cupboards.

Elizabethan and Jacobean herbalists, such as John Gerard, in his 'Herball or Historie of Plants' written in 1597, and John Parkinson in his 'Paradisum in sole paradisus terrestris' published in 1629, were mainly concerned with the medical, herbal or culinary uses of plants together with their cultivation. However, they noted resemblances between certain plants. Therefore, various species of delphinium and consolida were grouped together as 'larkes heals' or 'larkspurs' because it was thought that the centres of the florets resembled bird's feet. The scientific approach to botany, or the relationships between plants, as we think of it today, did not exist.

Our understanding of the development of plants and animals was revolutionised by Charles Darwin's theory of evolution, explained in his book 'On the origin of Species' published in 1859. We now know that every form of life on earth can be traced back to simple cells, which lived in the primeval soup aeons ago. From those, an increasingly complex tree of different forms of life can be traced. Then evolving and developing further and ever more diversely. The modern science of genetics is founded on Gregor Mendel's paper on the laws of inheritance, first read in 1865 but ignored by the scientific establishment until the early twentieth century.

The science of botany involves comparing and investigating specific features of plants together with the relationships between them. Studies of such relationships, aimed at developing a system of classification, are known as taxonomy. Botanical taxonomists systematically group related plants into families. Those, in turn, are split into sub-groups, referred to as genera, which contain individual species of plants that are more closely related to each other. Delphiniums are a single genus, or group, contained within the Ranunculaceae family, which includes many other genera such as hellebores, paeonies, aconitums and consolida (the annual larkspur).

Botanists use the binomial classification of plants, which predates Charles Darwin's theory of evolution. It consists essentially of giving a 'one word' name, such as *Delphinium* to a genus and a 'two word' name such as *Delphinium elatum* to an individual species within the genus. The system was established by Carl Linnaeus, the Swedish naturalist who provided a concise and use-able survey of the world's known plants and animals. About 7,700 species of plants were listed in his 'Species Plantarum' in 1753. Additionally, some 4,400 species of animals were listed separately in his 'Systema Naturae', in 1758.

Evolutionary change is an ongoing process so that considerable variation continues to occur amongst species. The differences are recognised, depending on their significance, as subspecies (written as subsp), varieties (var) or forma (f).

There are over 300 delphinium species that grow wild in the temperate zones of the Northern Hemisphere. They have a wide geographical range that extends across Europe, North Africa, Asia and North America. The important thing is that, despite their apparent differences, they are closely related. They evolved from a common ancestor that existed in the past when those four continents were connected.

Delphinium species as one might expect share certain similarities, such as spurred flowers usually set around racemes or flower spikes, although some are corymbose, with central bees or eyes. They also share fingered, lobed leaves. However, there are distinct variations in such things as height and size, individual flower features and colours as well as root systems that may be fibrous, tuberous or stoloniferous.

As a point of interest, delphiniums are unusual because there are species with red and yellow flowers in addition to the blues and purples. All three primary colours are represented in their blooms. There are also two African species with a strong and attractive scent.

Growing delphinium species is often challenging but can be very interesting. However, it must be admitted that many are not showy although some are. The best and most garden-worthy of them include the red flowered *D. nudicaule* and *D. cardinale*, the yellow *D. semibarbatum*, together with *D. tatsienense* and *D. grandiflorum*.

Careful selection of cultivated species has allowed greatly improved and very garden worthy seed strains, such as *D. grandiflorum* 'Blue Butterfly' to be developed. However, the key to obtaining major improvements in delphiniums must be to hybridise different species with a view to combining their most desirable characteristics.

Plants increase by sexual reproduction. That is to say that male pollen from one plant fertilises a female ovum contained in the flower of another similar plant. A hybrid is a plant that has genetically distinct parents, such as ones that belong to different species. However, the definition also embraces plants whose parents are different cultivars (or cultivated varieties, what most people used to describe simply as varieties).

Hybrids are denoted by placing an 'x' between the names of the two parents, prefaced by the name of the genus to which they belong. The parentage of species hybrids would be described as, for example, *D. cardinale x D. nudicaule*. In the case of cultivated varieties the names of the parent plants would be used, for example D. 'Blue Nile' x 'Loch Leven'.

It is possible for hybridisation to take place between delphinium species, within the same genus, due to their close relationship to each other. However, it cannot take place between plants from different genera, or groups of plants, within the Ranunculaceae family, such as delphiniums and buttercups, because their relationship is insufficiently close.

There are a number of reasons that different delphinium species do not normally hybridise in the wild. The most obvious is geographical location. There can be none occurring naturally between species in North America and those in Europe or Asia. Similarly, plants grow in distinct habitats or flower at different times. Where hybridisation does occur, the resulting plants may be infertile.

There are all sorts of barriers to hybridisation but the number of chromosomes contained within the cells of each parent plant is fundamental. Those must match for hybridisation to be able to take place. Chromosomes contain the basic genetic information that determines the way in which a plant will grow, and its final form.

Delphinium species are normally diploid, which is to say that each plant cell contains two sets of eight chromosomes, making sixteen in total. However mutations can occur naturally, very occasionally, or can be induced artificially in which the number of chromosomes is doubled, to create a tetraploid plant, having four sets of eight chromosomes per cell, making thirty-two in total.

Tetraploid plants are, usually, larger and stronger growing than diploid ones but since they do not usually cross-pollinate with the latter, they will always remain as a small proportion of wild populations of delphinium. On the rare occasions that hybridisation takes place between tetraploid and diploid plants, the resulting offspring will be triploids having 3 sets of 8 chromosomes, making 24 in total. Such plants (an example being most of the Belladonna delphinium hybrids) are normally sterile and do not set seed.

Plants have been collected from all parts of the world, and imported into Britain, for many years. Certainly, by the early 19th century, there were a number of delphinium species being grown. But, with confusing names, it is often difficult to determine which plants were which. What, for example, are we to make of 'Delphinium Formosum' which was introduced by Mr. G. Moore, a nurseryman from East Dereham, in Norfolk? It was widely grown but records are conflicting and it has been lost to cultivation. It was said to be a hybrid that came true from seed but there is an alternative suggestion, which is that it was a tetraploid selection of *D. elatum*. The plant was certainly distinct from, and predated, the true species *D. formosum*, from the Caucasus, which was identified in 1856 by Boissier and Huet. However, the latter is now considered to be of doubtful provenance and may, in fact, have been a violet flowered variation of *D. elatum*.

Hybridisation between the various species would have occurred naturally, if they were compatible and when grown close together. We believe that the earliest hybrid was the double, deep blue, 'Delphinium Barlowii', recorded in 1837, which was obtained from seed of *D. grandiflorum*, by a florist in Manchester. It was a popular plant, for many years, and was still listed by Kelways in 1881. We have no way of knowing if this, or any other early hybrid, was diploid or tetraploid.

The most important delphinium species, so far as plant breeders and hybridisers have been concerned, is *D. elatum*, a blue flowered alpine that is widely distributed from the Pyrenean mountain range to Siberia. It is fibrous rooted and grows on stony mountain slopes. The modern garden delphiniums include some obvious basic characteristics of that species, but are clearly hybrids.

The genesis of the elatum hybrid delphiniums, cultivated varieties or cultivars, for the garden is actually somewhat obscure since early records of the different species are poor, do not correspond with current nomenclature and are often confusing. Hybridisation may have occurred by chance but when deliberately carried out, by plant breeders, the details would very likely have been kept secret for commercial reasons. Since we weren't around at the time, we can only speculate. Therefore our account of the way in which the elatum hybrids were created is based on some theory and quite a lot of conjecture!

The modern, elatum hybrid delphiniums are tetraploid plants. They have twice the number of chromosomes in each plant cell than are present within those of the species. Nobody is sure how this came about. The most plausible explanation is that an increasing proportion of tetraploid plants would have been selected, because of their size and vigour, in cultivated species seed strains whilst the weakest growing plants, likely to be diploids, would have been discarded. Hybridisation could then have occurred between tetraploid rather than diploid species plants.

It is accepted that the Frenchman, Victor Lemoine, was responsible for creating the elatum hybrid delphiniums in about 1850. Nobody knows which plants, other than the species *D. elatum*, may have been involved in the original breeding but it is fun to speculate. It seems reasonable to suppose that popular garden plants, such as 'Delphinium Formosum' and 'Delphinium Barlowii', might have been involved if they were tetraploid hybrids. Certainly, 'Delphinium Barlowii versicolour' which is included in Lemoines 1857 list might have been the latter or a hybrid from it. Probable other candidates include tetraploid selections of a number of species, such as *D. grandiflorum*, *D. exaltatum* and *D. cheilanthum*.

Victor Lemoine, and his family, continued to breed delphiniums for many years, at his nursery, at Nancy in France. Their work culminated in the introduction of a plant named 'Statuaire Rude', first registered with the Royal Horticultural Society in 1906. It received an award of merit for exhibition in 1908 and a highly commended in 1917. It was notable for exceptionally large, for the time, heliotrope semi-double florets of up to 70 mm (2.75"), carried on spikes exceeding 0.6 mtrs (2'0") in length.

James Kelway, in England, imported a stock of Victor Lemoine's plants around 1859. It appears that George Phillips, writing his first book on delphiniums, was given access to Kelway's records. He tells us that although some hybridisation with species was tried, most of their breeding work was the result of deliberate hand pollinating and crossing of selected elatum hybrids. Kelways continued to raise and introduce delphiniums until the late 1920's. Probably their most famous plant was 'King of the Delphiniums', which was introduced in 1893. Its florets were coloured in a mixture of gentian blue and plum, with a white eye, carried on 0.6 mtr (2'0") spikes. It received an Award of Garden Merit in 1925.

Charles Langdon, a professional gardener, obtained a stock of plants from both Lemoine's and Kelway's nurseries. He gave an unflowered box of seedling delphiniums to A. A. Walters, a nurseryman from Bath, in 1896. It contained an outstanding delphinium, which was promptly named after Langdon's employer, the 'Reverend E. Lascelles'. It had violet florets and white eyes. It remains in cultivation but does not compare to more modern plants. Charles Langdon went into the nursery trade in 1901, in partnership with John Blackmore who was a friend with a specialist interest in begonias. Blackmore and Langdon remain as the leading delphinium nursery, to this day, having recently celebrated its centenary. Charles Langdon commenced a line breeding programme that was rigidly adhered to, by his successors, until the period between 1950 and 1960. Great emphasis was placed on selecting plants for toughness and perenniality as well as their more aesthetic qualities. That pedigree is one of the main reasons that the named cultivars have improved to such a spectacular extent. Notable plants, on which Blackmore and Langdon's breeding programme was based, include 'Millicent Blackmore' (1910) and 'Sir Douglas Haig' (1910). Other plants that were especially admired in their day include 'Bridesmaid' (1938), 'Silver Moon' (1960), 'Guy Langdon' (1960) and so many other great cultivars that it is impossible to list even a tiny fraction of them.

Delphinium breeding, in Britain, has to this day been aimed mainly at the production of a few exceptional selected cultivars, or clones, which can be propagated vegetatively from cuttings. The idea being that the plants, that result, will be exactly the same as their parents. It is possible, therefore, to select them for form, colour and size of florets, length of spike and so on. Having made those selections, the plants can then be trialled for a number of years, to ensure that their vigour, hardiness and perenniality is good before taking cuttings from them. By doing this, very reliable and tough garden plants can be grown and sold to the public which nurseries can guarantee will be true to type.

With the exception of the work done by Blackmore and Langdon, we think that little truly systematic delphinium breeding was carried out in Britain during the nineteenth and the early part of the twentieth century. But in America much work went on, from about 1920 onwards, to create seed strains. The reasons for the different approach are partly the gentle climate of the West Coast of America, giving insufficient winter rest for the plants, which can flower up to three times in a year. Long humid summers also make the plants more susceptible to diseases, which are unique to North America and warmer climates. Although delphiniums are perennial in the British and colder climates, they are not necessarily so in warmer countries.

Luther Burbank, Americas greatest plant breeder used seeds from British and French growers to produce his own strain of delphiniums, during the early twentieth century.

Edward Steichen was one of the most notable American delphinium breeders. His work commenced in France, in 1908, with elatum hybrids from Lemoine. He recorded that those had predominantly semi-double, mauve and lavender coloured flowers. He also obtained stock from Kelways, noting that their plants usually had smaller, single florets in dark blue. He continued to breed delphiniums in America, between the first and second world wars. However, his major contribution was the very successful hybridisation of a number of species, which led to the creation of the 'Connecticut Yankee' strain of bushy delphiniums. Edward Steichen was invited to stage a display of delphiniums at the Museum of Metropolitan Art in New York, in 1936. This was a great success and he considered it to be recognition of plant breeding as an art form, and the breeder as an artist.

Other early American breeders included Major Newel Vanderbilt, who is reputed to have achieved crosses between elatum hybrids, based on Luther Burbank's breeding, and *D. scopulorum var glaucum*, which is an American species. The plants raised by him were noted for their hard, slim and whippy stems. He also developed American inter-species hybrids.

One of the most notable, and interesting, breeding programmes was that of professor A. A. Samuelson, whose 'West o' the Rockies' seed strain was derived from American inter-species crosses centred, for the most part, around *D. nudicaule* and *D. menzeissii*. The plants were of dwarf habit, we understand tuberous rooted and with flowers in the widest possible range of colour which included white, yellow, red, pink as well as blue, purple and mauve. Unfortunately, the seeds were never marketed widely, if at all, and are now unavailable.

Professor Leon Leonian was a close contemporary of both Steichen and Vanderbilt. His original delphiniums derived from Victor Lemoine's breeding. He is reputed to have achieved exceptional plants with large mauve and lavender floret colours, on relatively short growing stems.

Charles Barber, of Troutdale, Oregon, an amateur raiser in the 1920's and 1930's, turned professional and built up a large commercial business. He originated the idea of seed selections with names. This resulted from the way in which his plants were classified as having light or dark florets, coupled with the colour of their eyes. Each separate classification was allocated to a letter of the alphabet, which then was named after a Red Indian tribe, for example 'Apache', 'Biloxi' and 'Cayuga'. However, Charles Barber's main contribution to the development of the delphinium was the introduction of the 'Hoodacre White' seed strain, emanating from a single albino plant that had, unlike countless others, good foliage. Scent also appeared in some of his white seedlings; selections of which included 'Odeur de Luxe', 'Angels Breath' and 'King Midas'.

Frank Reinelt was, for a time, the head gardener to Queen Marie of Romania. He emigrated to California in 1925, becoming the most important American breeder of elatum hybrid garden delphiniums, co-founding the firm of Vetterle and Reinelt in 1934. His 'Giant Pacific' strains of delphinium seed, with names usually inspired by Arthurian legend, provided plants in a 'Round Table' mixture of twelve separate ranges of colour that included magenta pinks, together with much more intense and bright blues and purples. These colour-breaks were a legacy of experimentation with *D. cardinale* and irradiation of its seeds, which doubled the chromosome count of its offspring, allowing them to be crossed with the elatum garden hybrids. Growing huge quantities of seedlings, with two generations each year in the warm Californian climate, he was able to produce plants that clearly surpassed British cultivars in terms of colour range and purity, plant architecture, floret size and formation.

We are not detracting from Frank Reinelt's great achievements when we say that his 'Giant Pacific' seedlings, and their descendants, have always been problematical in the British climate. It was never an objective to breed or test his plants for perenniality. To do so, in the gentle climate in which they were grown, was impossible. Therefore the constitution and hardiness, of plants grown from such seeds was, and remains, suspect. Frank Reinelt retired in 1969. So-called 'Giant Pacific' seed strains are still available, but do not resemble the originals. Most appear to have resulted from repeated selection of open-pollinated seeds (rather than Reinelt's procedure of hand crossing plants in one generation and saving open-pollinated seeds in the next) and have degenerated badly as a result. It is most unfortunate that inferior named 'Giant Pacific' seedlings are still the most commonly sold delphinium plants in garden centres.

In Britain, delphiniums probably attained their greatest popularity in the period between 1920 and 1940. Many nurseries, for example Hewitts of Stratford and Bees of Chester, specialised in them. They were responsible, in particular, for distributing Watkin Samuel's 'Wrexham' strain of so-called 'hollyhock' delphiniums, introduced in 1921. It was said that the spikes were massive, but mostly single flowered. His last introductions included 'Watkin Samuel' (1946), which had very modern looking light blue florets with dark eyes, that could only have derived from crosses with Reinelts Giant Pacific's. However, the poor constitution of the American strain had also been inherited.

Frank Bishop was a notable exhibitor and enthusiast who joined The Delphinium Society in 1929, shortly after it was formed. He became a professional delphinium breeder and worked for Bakers Nursery, at Codsall, who distributed the first list of Bishop delphiniums in 1946. He was inspired, in particular, to develop greatly improved blue delphiniums that would stand comparison with the mauves and purples in general cultivation at that time. We know that he crossed American 'Giant Pacific' seedlings with British cultivars, or his own seedlings, of known constitution and perenniality. By doing so, Frank Bishop opened up a variety of breeding opportunities, so that by the time he died, in 1957, the colour range of his delphinium cultivars had been widened considerably. Good whites such as 'Swan Lake' with its black eye, as well as very pale heliotropes, for example 'Cinderella', were added to the brilliant blues of 'Mrs Frank Bishop' and 'Betty Baseley'. A new 'Commonwealth strain' of delphiniums was also launched, having massive spikes with exceptionally large florets. Of those plants 'Ceylon', which is lavender with a white eye, remains in cultivation. Bakers, unfortunately, were a victim of a long running postal strike in 1970 which had a catastrophic effect on mail order nurseries, so that most of Frank Bishops cultivars were lost to the nursery trade.

The main European delphinium breeders have been the German Karl Foerster, who raised elatum type delphiniums of a distinctive type, mostly blue, single flowered and with hard stems. The Dutchmen Dr. Theodore Ruys and Dr Robert Legro, aimed to breed garden worthy red delphiniums. Dr. Ruys raised 'Pink sensation', introduced in 1936 and given an AM (g) by the R.H.S in 1941, was stated to be bred from a naturally occurring hybrid between D. nudicaule and an elatum hybrid. Starting in the early 1950's, Professor Robert Legro carried out an elaborate breeding programme that involved hybrids derived from cross-pollination between the garden elatum Delphiniums, the species D. nudicaule and also D. cardinale.

Frank Bishop's success, in crossing American 'Giant Pacific' seedling delphiniums with the tougher and more perennial British cultivars, was such that Blackmore and Langdon carried out a similar breeding programme to widen and improve certain colour ranges of their delphiniums. The results can be seen clearly in the brilliant blues of plants such as 'Blue Nile' and 'Fenella', bright purples such as 'Chelsea Star' as well as magenta pinks such as 'Turkish Delight' and 'Strawberry Fair'. Careful selection has ensured, however, that those plants have been hardy and long lasting.

Blackmore and Langdon also introduced a range of shorter growing named cultivars, based on breeding from a plant called 'Blue Tit' (1960). Those grow to between 1.1 and 1.4 mtrs (3'6" and 4'6") tall. They have proved to be hardy and perennial and are valuable plants for modern gardens, which are often small. Blackmore and Langdon also carried out a breeding programme, replicating that of Robert Legro, to incorporate red into the colour range of their delphiniums. Unfortunately their poor constitution, and a proneness to mildew, meant that the project was abandoned. Blackmore and Langdon made a commercial decision to cease large-scale delphinium breeding in 1978. However, they have continued to introduce new plants raised by amateur growers.

Many nurseries grew and bred delphiniums in Britain, before the second-world war. Their clientele included, mostly, owners of country houses with fashionable herbaceous borders. Changes in taste meant a decline in such gardens, together with the popularity of plants grown in them. This led, eventually, to the cessation of large-scale professional delphinium breeding.

It is a particular aim of The Delphinium Society to encourage the raising of new cultivars. This has become increasingly the preserve of amateur growers and breeders, such as Reg Lucas, Phil Milton, Jim Cooke, Ronnie Watts, Stuart Ogg, Clive Rowe, John Flowerday, Terry Murphy and Len Harrison.

Perhaps the first significant amateur grower was Ronald Parrett, his best known delphinium being the mid-blue 'Daily Express', a leading garden and exhibition plant for many years, obtained from a packet of the first batch of 'Bishop' delphinium seeds to be distributed by Baker's Nurseries. Others followed, mainly based on hybridisation between British cultivars and 'Giant Pacific' seed strains. Those included 'Demavand' (pale grey), 'Sunday Express' (white, flowering from 0.6 mtrs or 2'0" above the ground) and 'Taj Mahal' (cambridge blue with fawn eyes). Ronald Parrett championed shorter delphiniums for smaller gardens. His most interesting plant was possibly 'Dubonnet', growing no more than 0.66 mtrs (or 2'6") high, a dark wine colour with perfectly proportioned spikes and florets. It was a model of its type; unlike many modern dwarf seedlings which have overlarge florets on short stubby spikes. Ronald Parrett was an important Delphinium Society member having been instrumental in reviving its fortunes during the 1950's and pioneering a new style yearbook that was a sensation for its time.

Colin Edwards' delphinium breeding activities took off in earnest after his early retirement. He obtained permission to grow seedlings on a plot of ground near his home. He subsequently introduced a number of new cultivars, in conjunction with Ian Butterfield who is a professional nurseryman. Colin's best-known plants are probably 'Claire' (short growing pink with fawn eyes), named after his daughter in law, and the mid-blue, white eyed 'Joan Edwards' named after his wife.

Tom Cowan was a Scotsman who embarked on a quest for pure blue and turquoise delphiniums. The former resulted in the 'Loch' series, which included

'Loch Nevis,' a towering mid-blue exhibition cultivar, which dominated Delphinium Society shows for many years. 'Loch Leven', from the same hand-cross, is a shorter growing light blue cultivar. 'Spindrift' and 'Gossamer' are mauve with a hint of turquoise. His white delphiniums, 'Rona' and 'Iona', both have a green tinge. A number of Delphinium Society members were encouraged and inspired by him to start a breeding programme. In the late 1970's he established the breeders sub-committee of the Delphinium Society and this encouraged another generation of amateur breeders, many of whom are still active today.

Roy Latty took early retirement to become more deeply involved in delphinium breeding, operating a small nursery from his home at Ashton Deanland, during the 1970's, where he raised many fine cultivars. Those included 'Rosina' and 'Summer Wine', both of which were magenta pinks, 'Florestan' which is mauve with large and prominent dark eyes, 'Snowdon' with steely grey florets set off by a fawn eye. Two of his introductions, in particular, have stood the test of time, those being 'Sandpiper', which is white with a dark brown eye, and 'Leonora' which is a clear and bright mid-blue colour with white eyes.

Duncan McGlashan has been breeding delphiniums for a considerable time, developing seed strains in Holland, but also as an amateur raising named cultivars in Britain. Outstanding plants raised by him include 'Lucia Sahin', 'Min', 'Bruce' and 'Atholl'.

Nigel Moody has raised a number of plants including 'Sunkissed', 'Purple Velvet' and 'Blue Lagoon'. Henry Wilkins has also raised a number of cultivars including 'Walton Gemstone'.

David and Shirley Bassett are the well-known breeders of many exceptional and good quality delphinium cultivars, including for example, 'Galileo', 'Rosemary Brock', 'Lilian Bassett' and 'Summerfield Oberon'.

The Woodfield brothers introduced a significant number of worthwhile cultivars, in recent years, from their nursery near Stratford-on-Avon. Those include 'Clifford Sky', 'Clifford Pink' and 'Anne Woodfield'. There are, In addition, a number of delphinium cultivars that have been introduced recently, by Rougham Hall Nurseries.

The elatum hybrid garden delphinium is usually thought to be the quintessence of a British flower. However, its pedigree is really very cosmopolitan, with major contributions having been made, we suggest in equal proportion, by French, American and British breeders.

CHAPTER TWO

DELPHINIUMS AT THE START OF THE 21st CENTURY

By Duncan McGlashan, Kees Sahin and John Thirkell

This chapter has three main aims. The first is to review what hybridisers have achieved during the past 50 years, especially in terms of plant architecture as well as the range and quality of colour. The second aim is to review critically what has been attempted by raisers but not so far achieved, such as the obvious one of a wider colour range including deep reds, true pinks and yellows. In the context of these two aims, the third is to discuss what might possibly, be achieved by raisers in the framework of the next three decades.

Plant architecture is the term used to characterise the structure, size and proportion of the plant together with the form of the spike and the florets that compose it. There are still some cultivars, which are tall at say 1.9 mtrs (6'3") but many of the best pre-1950 cultivars were bigger and often started to flower very high on the stem. There has been significant improvement in this aspect. On many of the more recent introductions, though not all, the flower spike begins lower down even on taller plants. In terms of spike architecture there has been steady progress and the majority of cultivars introduced over the last few decades have good symmetry. This reflects, in general, a preference for pyramidal spikes, broad at the base and tapering gracefully to the top of the spike rather than the columnar shape that was once the general rule.

Floret sizes of 82mm (3.25") are now commonplace but perhaps of more importance the substance of the florets, texture and form including placement, shows considerable progress. Similarly the inner or eye petals are bigger and neater with a much wider range of colours giving some very striking floret/eye effects. Perhaps the floret classes at the Delphinium Society shows have led to greater awareness of the form and substance of florets as important criteria when selecting new plants.

In the latter period of the 20th century the need for more short cultivars was widely accepted. Blackmore and Langdon introduced 'Blue Tit' and some other shorter cultivars in about 1960. Bakers also introduced shorter growing plants, such as 'H. G. Mills', from their Codsall nursery. The expectation was that this would lead to a significantly wider range of such plants but, although some have been introduced, the number is far fewer than might have been expected. Experience with seedling strains promoted as dwarf has shown that, although in the first year the plants were shorter, they have been much taller when grown on in subsequent years. This is not the case with the pygmies developed by McGlashan and Sahin. However, it is clear that controlled spike/height requires systematic selection, given that it is important to ensure that the shorter plants remain so when they are over

2 years old, as well as being in proportion in terms of spike to stem ratio and floret size.

Extending the colour range of delphiniums has long been a major aim of breeders. There has been substantial progress in improvement especially of self-colours, fewer of what Tom Cowan used to call 'football Jerseys'! There have been substantial improvements in the quality and brightness of the colours, in particular blues. A significant factor is judged to be the influence of Reinelt's 'Giant Pacific' hybrids which were a landmark in the quality of seed strains. However, the perenniality of the American seed strains was always doubtful. They were used for hybridising with the British cultivars but their influence on those has always been problematic because some of the latter have shown a reduction in perenniality. On the bonus side, the incorporation of the 'Giant Pacific' blood has allowed a widening of the available colour ranges. In particular, the magenta pink colourings that are now so popular, as well as the creams, which appear to be linked genetically to those, could not have been obtained. The early pinks were often of poor constitution and in the main not very clear in colour. Since the 1950's there has been considerable improvement, especially in the deeper pinks, 'Rosemary Brock' and 'Lucia Sahin' reflecting this. In terms of white cultivars there is now a good range available. We also now have some good light creamy yellows such as 'Sungleam' and 'Sunkissed'.

Unfortunately although the fifty years work by Bob Legro on the University Hybrids produced major improvements in red colours, salmon pinks and some true yellows, these have not proved reliably hardy, although in Holland they are grown under glass for the cut flower market. How they would perform in a different climate corresponding more to the West Coast of America, where the red species come from, is a matter for conjecture. It remains true that in the modern delphinium we have one of the widest colour ranges of any group of plants, especially in blue, although true turquoise remains elusive.

Future Prospects

Without doubt the most interesting work on delphiniums during the 20th century was the hybridising carried out by Bob Legro and others including Leonian, Melqhuist, Samuelson, Steichen and Vanderbilt. They crossed a wide range of delphinium species with elatum hybrids. The work on *D. cardinale, D.nudicaule* and *D. semibarbatum* was of special interest because of the intriguing prospect of good red and yellow delphiniums. Ironically, at the start of the 21st century, most hybridisers appear to have abandoned work with those species. For the moment future prospects depend upon work within the elatum and also the Belladonna hybrids, whilst there remains breeding potential in Edward Steichen's 'Connecticut Yankee' types. Perhaps too genetic manipulation could be used, though for the moment that is unlikely by reason of the sheer cost of scientific resources. At the moment there is also considerable general antipathy to the use of genetic manipulation in any field. It could be said that such attitudes may prove to be based upon prejudice and that perhaps a more considered approach will develop over time.

Possible Aims

A ~ Plants in General:

1. To improve perenniality for which, at present, no truly adequate assessment system exists.
2. To achieve a wider range of height. In particular we need more short cultivars down to say 0.6 mtrs (2'0") with whippy stems that require little or no staking. Such plants should also remain in proportion in terms of total height/spike ratio. That is to say that the reduction in size should include both spike and florets.
3. To achieve an improvement of foliage. Many existing cultivars show a rather tatty appearance, post flowering, especially low on the plant. The leaves of yellow or cream cultivars suffer from an ochre tinge that is unattractive.
4. To improve slug and snail resistance, by producing plants of lower appeal to these pests, possibly by increasing silica content of leaves and shoots. This would probably require genetic manipulation. Also to develop effective biological methods using bacteria and parasites.
5. Improved general resistance to bacterial, fungal and viral attack is needed, especially in respect of mildew.
6. Resistance to eelworms (especially pratylenchus spp) needs to be improved. Safe and effective chemical controls are needed, since at present the only effective agents are much too toxic for general use.

B ~ Flowers

1. To further extend the colour range both of florets and eyes, in particular into deep yellows, salmon, red, green tinted and brown/black shades in both. Also new floret/eye contrasts; for example blue or pink eyes on white or cream florets. Also, veining and suffusion effects.
2. To increase the number of good quality seed strains which come true to colour. These exist for light blue, white and purple in F1 generations but the F2 are unproven. To ensure that these seeds are stored properly and made available through normal retail outlets.
3. To replace the commonly grown, but inferior, 'Giant Pacific' seedling plants sold by garden centres with ones grown from superior seed strains.
4. To develop multiple layers of petals for double flowers and/or crenated and fimbriated florets to add to the plants appeal for flower arrangers.
5. To increase the period that plants remain in full bloom, perhaps by slower setting of seeds, by plants that throw spikes at intervals or by increased branching of laterals, which then should flower over an extended period.
6. To find a cheap and safe treatment for cut spikes, so that these magnificent flowers could be used for cut flower purposes by the average gardener or flower arrangers. In particular, if delphinium laterals lasted seven days or so, they would surely be very popular in floral arrangements.
7. To breed named cultivars with an attractive perfume. Anyone who has grown seedlings on a large scale may have noticed the odd one with slight fragrance. By using these, together with the scented species, *D. leroyi* and *D. wellbyi*, it is possible that we could at long last have a scented named cultivar that would surely be of considerable appeal to gardeners at large.

Lastly, whether all the possible aims outlined will be achieved during the 21st century is open to question. What we are sure of is that our magnificent flower will remain 'Queen of the Border'.

The first four photographs, on the following pages, illustrate the progress in breeding new and improved delphinium cultivars during the last 150 years.

The wild species Delphinium elatum growing in the Swiss Alps: All delphinium cultivars have been developed from hybridisation between this and other species. *Photograph by kind permission of Pete Murray/PM-iMAGES.*

The 'Reverend E. Lascelles': Raised by A. A. Walters of Bath. The plant originated from a box of unflowered seedlings given to him by Charles Langdon. Blackmore and Langdon introduced the plant in 1907, when it received an Award of Merit from the Royal Horticultural Society. The florets are quite small whilst the spikes are narrow and columnar.

'Eva Gower': Raised and introduced by Frank Bishop in 1941. It received an Award of Garden Merit in 1945. You can see from studying the photograph that the florets show a significant advance in terms of both size and form. The clarity of colour has improved and the plant is a really good blue. The spikes show a significant increase in length but remain columnar in shape. This plant, in common with other delphiniums of the time, was very tall, in excess of 2.13 mtrs or 7'6".

'Galileo': One of the latest plants to be introduced, from David and Shirley Bassett. The florets show considerable improvement in size and form, whilst the spikes, which are pyramidal in shape, extend from half way up the plant. It has performed well at the Wisley Trials held by the Royal Horticultural Society.

The next four pictures illustrate the wide colour range of delphiniums:

'Summerfield Miranda': Raised, by David and Shirley Bassett, is an excellent pale pink for the garden and exhibition. The form of the florets, set off by dark eyes, is extremely nice.

'Giotto': Also raised by David and Shirley Bassett and is an attractive mauve with sharply defined blue bars at the centre of each sepal. Once again, a good plant that performs well.

'Anne Woodfield': Has very attractive blue tinted silvery flowers. It was raised and introduced by the Woodfields' Nursery.

'Tiger Eye': Raised and introduced by Bob Banks. This is an outstanding modern mauve cultivar with an exceptional black and gold eye.

The wild species *Delphinium elatum* growing in the Swiss Alps

The 'Reverend E. Lascelles'

'Eva Gower'

'Galileo'

'Summerfield Miranda'

'Giotto'

'Anne Woodfield'

'Tiger Eye'

CHAPTER THREE

DELPHINIUMS IN THE GARDEN

By Les Cooper

During the summer delphiniums are wonderful plants for turning the most ordinary of gardens into something special. Their colours are eye-catchingly beautiful without being garish. The height of the spikes dominates flower borders but does not overwhelm them. There is no doubt that a group of delphiniums grown well provides an impact that will always command attention. Look at photographs taken in famous gardens during June or July and nine times out of ten delphiniums will be there somewhere. Undoubtedly they are indispensable flowers for the summer garden. The question is how are they best used?

Delphiniums in specialised beds

Within the Delphinium Society quite a number of enthusiasts have beds containing nothing but delphiniums. When in flower no one can deny that these beds are startlingly dramatic providing a whole mass of colour. Gardeners who have seen the Delphinium Trials at Wisley gardens will know just how spectacular a large group of delphiniums can be. Anyone who specialises in hybridising or exhibiting them likes to grow a lot of plants and therefore have beds devoted solely to their favourite. However, there are problems with this approach especially if only a small garden is available. The main objection being that the bed will only look good for six weeks or so in the year. During the rest of the time there is not a lot to see. There are other factors too, which can cause problems. Slugs and snails love delphinium shoots and a group of delphiniums provide a banquet for them. Similarly with caterpillars, whose parents can home in to the collection to lay their eggs. Naturally plants will be prone to pests even if they are grown amongst others in a border but they will be less of a target.

Delphiniums in borders

More normally delphiniums are grown with other plants in borders. They have long been a favourite within the traditional herbaceous border where the tall delphiniums usually get featured at the back. They are also associated with the old English cottage gardens, which is a bit laughable when you read of their history. Nowadays mixed borders or cottage garden beds are more common. These are borders that have all types of plants and bulbs grown together. Let's look at some of the assets that delphiniums can bring to such a border.

Colour

I suppose the thing that attracts most of us to delphiniums is the colour. Many people think in terms of "geraniums red and delphiniums blue" and for lots of gardeners the prime attraction is their blue colour. After all blue is not that common in the plant world and it shows up so well against the many greens of the surrounding foliage. Chocolate box pictures of cottage gardens, with pink roses, blue delphiniums and blue skies linger in all our memories. So, frequently, the variety of colours found amongst the modern cultivars can surprise those new to gardening and who are not familiar with delphiniums. A glance through this book will give a good idea of the range to choose from. White, cream, pink, mauve, blue, violet and purple cultivars are all available. Then again the eyes or bees can differ tremendously with, for example, some whites having white eyes, others shades of brown while some have black. Another point to make is that all delphinium colours are cool shades and there is nothing garish about them. It is fair to say that there are delphiniums to suit any garden colour scheme.

Height

In general modern elatum delphiniums are reasonably tall plants that usually grow around 1.6 mtrs (about 5'6"), high and there are a few that reach over 1.8 mtrs (6'0"). Thankfully, the days have long since passed when herbaceous borders were full of monstrous delphiniums with spikes in excess of 2.4 mtrs (8'0") which often had lots of stem and some bloom at the top. Now the flowers start just above the foliage with florets that hold their petals much longer. Raisers, too, have produced some shorter cultivars that can be very useful in providing a variation in height. However, some people regard any tall plants as not suitable for the small garden. Many are the times I have heard people say "I love delphiniums but I've only got a little garden". What nonsense; most small gardens fail because their owners think they can only grow tiny plants. What is needed is height. Delphiniums are ideal because they grow tall and give lots of bloom without taking up half the garden.

Form

Most modern elatum delphiniums are pyramidal, in that the flower spike is broader at the base than the top. In most people's opinion this gives a more elegant look. Older cultivars tended to be more columnar and look somewhat less attractive. Nevertheless, delphiniums are very architectural looking flowers providing an impact rather like that which church spires and towers make in the English country landscape. I would stress that only the best seeds and plants will produce the best. Breeding matters so much.

Length of season

The amount of time that a delphinium is in flower is surprisingly long. First the main flowers come out and then, when these are over and they're cut off, the laterals come into their own extending the season.

Some cultivars flower earlier or later than others so that if a group is carefully selected with some early cultivars, some mid-season and some later flowering, then the flowering period can be increased by at least four weeks. The catalogues of specialist delphinium growers will always give the flowering period usually as early, mid-season or late.

If after flowering the dead flower stems are cut down just below the bottom florets then occasionally the plants will flower again. One of the merits of Belladonna Hybrids is that they will nearly always give a second display if they are cut back following their initial summer flowering.

Maintenance

If you are planning to have a low maintenance garden then probably delphiniums will not feature very high on the list of plants to grow. This is principally because they will certainly require staking. Even Belladonna delphiniums, which are shorter and bushier, usually require some form of support. At least you know where you stand with delphiniums. Many if not most perennials which are, allegedly, easy to maintain have to be propped up following the breezes of early summer. No, any gardener knows delphiniums have to be staked. Many also know that it's a price worth paying.

The one thing that everyone knows about delphiniums is that they are the favourite food of slugs and snails. In reply, I merely repeat what I have said and point out that many plants suffer in a similar way. Hostas are, if anything, worse because they get eaten throughout their growing season. Delphiniums suffer most in the dormant season and early spring when the new shoots inevitably get chewed unless action is taken. Things like new clematis shoots or lettuce seedlings suffer in a similar fashion but this doesn't stop people from growing them. The fact is that slugs and snails are a problem for many plants in the garden and there is nothing to stop anyone from growing delphiniums provided they protect their plants soon enough.

Post flowering

Even the most besotted delphinium enthusiast would be hard put to describe a delphinium plant after flowering as elegant. Once the flower spike has been cut off below the last dead floret and the leaves begin to deteriorate then it really needs hiding. Easier said than done but in an ideal border there should be later flowering plants, perhaps kniphofia or aster frikartii to mask the offenders.

Making the best of your delphiniums

So delphiniums have lots going for them but how are they to be used to best effect? In many respects this is up to you and your taste. Gardens are meant to mirror the personality of their owners and, after all, it's your patch of soil. The best way to learn is to look at other people's gardens. Often you find out what not to do as well as what to do to get good results. Nevertheless, there are a few pointers that might help.

Location

It is useful to make, at least, a rough plan of the intended garden layout. This has to be practical. It's pointless to say "delphiniums would look wonderful there", without first thinking about the location. First visualise their requirements. Delphiniums need at least half a day in the sun. To place them in the shade or under a tree just asks for failure. A very dry area is, also, not good. So choose somewhere in the open. Then make sure the soil is fertile and replete with humus. Prepare the border well before planting. There is nothing worse than a half starved and neglected delphinium.

I know of many gardeners going to garden centres where they see a plant and feel the urge to buy it. The trouble is when they get home there is the question of where to put it. We all do this but it's not the best way to achieve that perfect garden. Decide where the delphiniums can be grown best and then get the plants.

Groups

A single delphinium plant looks nice but is a little isolated in a border, whereas a group in full bloom looks fantastic. I would suggest a minimum of three and stick to odd numbers if you go for more. If possible, use a group of the same cultivar because it gives a bolder effect.

Companion plants

The question of which plants look best with delphiniums is impossible for me to answer sensibly. For a start it all depends on the eye of the beholder and I might like flowers that another person hates. Secondly, I'm prejudiced and tend to think that anything goes with delphiniums. Thirdly, my views change from season to season and this year's favourite could be my next year's duffer. But nothing daunted I will set out some of my thoughts.

Because I have a fairly small garden I can't be bothered overmuch with trying to have an all the year round display. Instead I aim for three main peak periods of bloom; early spring with daffodils and tulips (mostly in pots and containers); autumn with michaelmas daisies, dahlias, heleniums, anemones and crocosmia, and of course summer with delphiniums. I do like to see something in flower during the winter just to raise my spirits. But quite honestly over the last few years the weather has been so dreary that I spend as little time out in the garden as possible and then concentrate my efforts on preparing for the summer and autumn display.

The star of the summer is the delphinium and when you are interested in them the problem becomes one of trying not to grow too many. Roses seem to be a natural companion and especially some of the old ones like 'Penelope', 'Cornelia' and 'Buff beauty,' also the newer 'English Roses' from David Austin like 'Abraham Darby' and 'Graham Thomas'; These soft and paler shades of pink and apricot work so well with the delphinium shades of blue and mauve.

The list of hardy perennials that flower at more or less the same time as delphiniums is endless. There are many new colours in the achillea family. A favourite is campanula lactiflora 'Loddon Anna' a superb pale pink perennial that sets off the brighter delphiniums. Coreopsis verticulata flowers for weeks on end. There are scores of beautiful hemerocallis cultivars that would grace any garden. Similarly, there are many hardy geraniums to choose from but I would recommend 'Roxanne', blue with a white centre, and 'Patricia' a tallish bright pink. Monardas are a favourite of mine and, again, there are several newish varieties on the market. The same applies to heuchera and heucheralla that have improved immensely. I could go on and on but undoubtedly the best way to choose plants is to see them growing and I sincerely recommend seeing the borders at the R.H.S. Gardens at Wisley, Surrey.

The use of colour in borders is a subject that would fill another book. Not having that amount of space I guess that for me it boils down to two choices. Do I want contrasting companions for my delphiniums or do I want complementary ones? Gertrude Jekyll grew orange lilies with deep blue delphiniums and felt that it was successful. I dare not argue and remember well a beautiful garden where a similar use was made with orange inulas. With the more cobalt shades I rather like the yellow coreopsis verticulata mentioned previously. In a way these warm and cool contrasts are easier to manage due to the fact that there are a lot of yellows and oranges available at the time the delphiniums flower.

As usual it's down to your own tastes but I rather like complementary companions because the warmth of summer just begs for cool borders. With all the green foliage in the garden at that time you're half way there and drifts of delphiniums, pink roses, monardas and sidalceas make a real picture.

A border from seed

Named delphiniums are not cheap to buy. One named delphinium will set you back £5 or more. The reason is simple ..... named cultivars are propagated by taking cuttings. This is a fiddly task and a time consuming one too. Hardy perennial plants are expensive also although not all of them come from cuttings or micro-propagation. Quite a number of the plants on sale in garden centres are raised from seed. This includes the delphiniums sold under Arthurian names such as 'Galahad' or 'Astolat.'

It is a lot cheaper for anyone wishing to start a mixed border or restock an old one to grow their own delphiniums and other hardy perennials. With a little bit of effort and attention you can obtain a really good border by growing the plants from seed. This will save you quite a bit of money and in many instances give you plants identical to those bought from a garden centre. This excludes delphiniums because those grown from seed obtained from a specialist delphinium source will be far superior to the garden centre versions. As explained elsewhere in this book, delphiniums are quite easy to grow from seed. A packet will supply all your needs. Many other perennials are just as easy although some will take longer before they flower. Another advantage is that it enables you to grow plants rarely seen in garden centres or nurseries.

A white border

Anyone who ever goes to Vita Sackville West's garden at Sissinghurst always remembers the white border. This could be great fun to create in your own garden and there are some excellent white delphiniums available to help make an eye-catching display. 'Elizabeth Cook' a white with white eye is a wonderful delphinium. 'Sandpiper' and 'Atholl' have dark eyes; 'Olive Poppleton' a honey coloured eye. 'Lilian Bassett' also has a black eye but grows a little shorter than average. Delphiniums are very suitable for a white garden because of their architectural form and the subtle shades of white and near white that are available.

Island beds

These were popular in the 1950's but are now seldom mentioned. From a delphinium grower's point of view they are not a bad idea because they enable the delphiniums to be in the open and not stuck against a wall or hedge where they do not get enough sun or moisture.

CHAPTER FOUR

CULTIVATION

By Patrick Booth and Allan Cook

A well-grown bed of delphiniums is a magnificent sight, a good example being the trials at the Royal Horticultural Society's gardens at Wisley, in Surrey. Their plants are grown to the very highest standard, with bloom spikes up to 1.2 mtrs (4'0") long and measuring up to 0.3 mtrs (1'0") across their bases. Many wonder if some magic ingredients have been used to grow such beautiful plants and to keep them upright. There is, of course, none involved; just lots of manure and compost, regular watering, tender loving care together with canes and twine. However, it must be conceded that such plants are exceptional, the cultivation methods needed to achieve the very best display possible are perhaps more representative of growing for exhibition than the garden.

Most people are impressed when they see such magnificent plants, but dismiss the idea of growing delphiniums for themselves because they think they are too big and tall for their gardens. This is not, however, necessarily the case. If less extreme cultivation methods are followed, the delphiniums will not be of exhibition size but will still be impressive enough for most tastes, and will be more manageable, weather and disease resistant, as well as longer lived.

If you cultivate delphiniums, the foundations for success are always laid by good ground preparation. This is vital because they will be required to grow and flower for a number of years. Therefore, incorporating liberal quantities of well-rotted manure, or compost, into the soil is strongly recommended. In other respects, there are significant differences to the way in which you treat your plants, depending on whether you are growing for exhibition or the garden.

Growing delphiniums for exhibition involves the use of highly nitrogenous fertilisers, especially during the early part of the growing season. The plants will grow larger and more luxuriantly as a result, but if too much fertiliser is used the results are likely to be misshapen or very coarse looking spikes. The skill of growing plants for show is to judge just how much feeding can be given, without overdoing things. The disadvantages of a high nitrogen diet are that the plants will have softer growth and be less weather resistant, more prone to bacterial and fungal diseases that attack the crown and roots, and therefore shorter lived.

If you prefer to grow your delphiniums for garden display, rather than for exhibition, they should be grown 'hard'. That is to say that excessive use of nitrogenous fertilisers should be avoided. Whilst the plants will benefit from moderate use of these in the spring, the emphasis should be more on using 'balanced' formulations containing equal proportions of nitrogen, phosphates and potash. During the latter part of the season, high potash type fertilisers, which also contain high levels of phosphate, would be more appropriate, in order to harden the plants off before the winter.

Food is not the only important key to success. Delphiniums are substantial plants that grow rapidly but are relatively shallow rooted. Therefore you should make sure that your plants are adequately watered at all times, although continuous use of seep hoses should be avoided because it is likely to cause crown rot and other problems more usually associated with growing plants in boggy ground.

The elatum hybrid delphinium is a hardy herbaceous perennial plant. That is to say that it grows through the spring and summer, flowering in June or July and then setting seed. Foliage dies back in the late summer and autumn. During the winter the crown and roots remain intact, below ground. New growth emerges in the spring. The cycle repeats for a number of years.

Some delphiniums are more perennial than others. Short-lived plants might last for three or four years. Good ones should persist for well over ten. A distinction must be made between perenniality and hardiness. Delphiniums are very hardy and resistant to frost and can be over wintered in very cold climates such as Iceland, Canada or Alaska.

An elatum hybrid garden delphinium consists of a hard 'crown', which is quite woody in older plants and lies just below ground level. Stems, leaves and flower spikes grow from the sides and top. Fibrous 'feeder' roots grow down and out to a diameter of about 0.75 mtrs (2'6"). The harder the crown, generally speaking, the greater the longevity and disease resistance of the plant will be. In other words, it will be more perennial.

Older delphiniums develop strong 'anchor' roots that grow deep into the soil and give stability to the plants. Those in particular resent disturbance. We believe that if they are cut or broken they do not re-grow. Therefore you should avoid moving older plants if at all possible, since they are unlikely to recover, but if you do have to move large plants we recommend really thorough watering in with a sprinkler.

New 'eyes', or buds, are formed on the top and sides of the crown, during the growing season. Those remain dormant over the winter. New shoots grow from them in the following spring. It is the eyes and young shoots, that slugs and snails so love to eat and which, therefore, need protecting.

Leaves have seven lobes and serrated edges. Their colour will give a good, quick visual check of the overall health of a plant. They should be a good, deep green. Yellowing is an indication of poor health. An exception to this general rule is that the leaves and stems of cream flowered delphiniums always have a shiny ochre colour; not pretty, but quite normal.

Delphinium stems are hollow. Some plants have thicker and fleshier ones than others. They should ideally be hard, slim and whippy. The bases, where they join the crown, should also be solid and hard, giving good wind and weather resistance; but also making it easier to strike cuttings in the spring.

Flower spikes consist of a series of florets; each set on a pedicel (an individual short side stem). The florets should be arranged in spirals around the main stem. Lateral flowering shoots develop from just below the bases of the main spikes. They flower after, prolonging the display.

Male (pollen bearing anthers) and female (receptive stigma, style and ovaries) reproductive organs are at the centre of each floret and are surrounded, or guarded, by an eye (the true petals). Those, in turn, are surrounded by one or more rows of coloured sepals (formed from the casing of the flower bud). Just to be confusing, everyone refers to the sepals as petals and to the petals as 'the eye': logical, because that is what they look like, but technically incorrect.

Situation

Delphiniums prefer an open situation, which allows air to circulate around the plants. Sunshine helps the stems to harden.

A close situation under trees is not recommended because it encourages fungal diseases such as mildew. It tends to make delphiniums grow taller and weaker. Some degree of partial shading can however be tolerated, although the plants will be drawn up and will have loosely formed spikes.

Roots from trees, hedges and shrubs will rob the surrounding soil of both water and nutrients. Therefore, delphiniums grown in their vicinity will need extra watering and feeding. Any hedges and shrubs should be kept trimmed back as far as possible to reduce their demand for food and water.

It is of particular importance that delphiniums should be planted in a well-drained situation. They do not tolerate being planted in waterlogged ground since this will cause the crown and roots to rot during the winter.

Soil preparation

Delphiniums prefer a neutral, loamy soil but are tolerant of most types. If you are moving to a new garden it is, of course, advisable to have the soil tested. You should prepare the ground thoroughly, especially if it is a hungry sandy or chalky type. Nutrients leach quickly from such soils so that regular use of fertilisers will be necessary. Irrespective of the soil type, you should incorporate good well-rotted manure or compost, before planting delphiniums or anything else. The plants respond well to good cultivation and like a substantial diet. Double digging (that is, to the depth of two spades) should not, normally, be necessary but will depend on the types of soil and sub-soil. Delphiniums primarily, are surface rooting. Therefore, burying manure or compost deeply is unlikely to benefit the plant to any major extent. It may be that the drainage of clay, or clay subsoil, can be improved in this way, but if there is no over riding reason that flower beds should be double dug, then there is no point in undertaking it. It is important that the soil should be dug and prepared well in advance, giving time for it to settle before any planting is carried out.

What you remove from the soil, before planting, is at least as important as what you incorporate. When preparing beds for delphiniums, or any other kinds of flower, ensure that tenacious perennial weeds are dug out or killed. In Britain, those include such things as couch grass, bindweed, ground elder, and celandine. Bindweed, for example, is so deep rooted that you cannot dig it out. If you have a serious problem then we suggest that you should prepare the beds in the autumn, incorporating manure or compost. Use a glyphosate based systemic weed killer, such as 'Roundup', on weeds in the autumn. This should be followed by an application of a paraquat based weedkiller such as 'Weedol'. Leave the bed to lie fallow and then treat emerging weed shoots in the following spring using several applications of the same weed killers. New planting can then be carried out from May or June onwards. All weed killers are nasty substances and should be treated with respect. Always use rubber gloves and follow the manufacturer's instructions and recommended precautions exactly.

Planting

Delphiniums can, theoretically, be planted at any time during the growing season.

Nurseries used to despatch large rooted cuttings during the early autumn but this had the disadvantage that they were unable to become fully established during the winter. The normal practice, nowadays, is for small rooted cuttings to be potted on and sold between May and early July. This is an ideal time to plant young delphiniums. One specialist delphinium nursery, at least, has also sold small 'plug' plants in the spring, which in our experience have grown well.

If you have an opportunity to inspect young rooted cuttings, before purchase, and certainly before planting, there are some things that should be checked. Firstly, while it is important that there should be a good root system, be careful to see that the young plants are not pot-bound. If they are, they should be avoided. However, if you have no alternative, you can tease the roots apart. You must also ensure that the tip of the primary shoot has had its top pinched out and that, most importantly, new shoots are breaking from the base of the plant. This is absolutely vital. Do not buy the delphinium, or plant it in any circumstances, before that has occurred.

You should dig an ample planting hole. A couple of handfuls of fertiliser, such as blood, fish and bone, should be incorporated into it. The correct planting depth will be evident if the delphinium is growing in a container. If not, then the top of the plant's crown should be fractionally below soil level. It is important that, after planting, the soil should be firmed gently around the delphiniums. The plants should then be watered in well. Even when the planting has been carried out carefully, the delphiniums should be checked a couple of days later, to ensure that the correct planting levels have been achieved.

Delphiniums are big plants, requiring a lot of space to grow. It is recommended that they should be planted 0.75 to 1 mtrs (2'6" to 3'0") apart. This will leave sufficient space for you to weed, stake and generally look after them. It should also be said that, if your delphiniums are planted too closely together, then this is likely to encourage mildew and other fungal diseases.

An alternative to planting directly into the ground is to transplant your delphiniums into large pots for growing on. This has the advantage that they are well established before planting out, later in the year. Delphiniums can be over-wintered for planting out in the following spring, if necessary, which could be an advantage if you have to take a long time to prepare the flower beds, but you must take care that they do not become pot bound. Be prepared to transfer the plants to larger pots if you have to.

Once planting has been carried out, it is important that your delphinium named cultivars, or special seedlings, are labelled clearly so you know what they are. It is best to purchase long labels that can be inserted deep into the soil at the base of the plant. An alternative is to push the tapered ends of your labels into the holes, at the tops of canes surrounding your plant.

Growing on

Young plants can be of two basic types. The first category being 'named cultivars' which have been propagated from cuttings, either obtained from delphinium specialist nurseries or ones you have taken yourself. The second category is seedlings, which will include virtually any plant obtained from a garden centre.

Named delphinium cultivars are, of course, a known quantity in terms of colour, height and form, so that the grower knows what to expect. Therefore it makes perfect sense that they should be planted out into their final flowering positions as soon as they are large enough.

In the case of seedling plants, however, the situation is slightly different insofar as those will always vary in terms of quality, colour and desirability. Therefore, they should be planted out into seedling beds and grown on to the point at which their merits can be assessed. Desirable plants should then be retained and planted out into their final positions within the garden. Those that are poor should, obviously, be discarded.

Small seedling delphiniums can be planted very close together, initially, perhaps 0.3 mtrs (1'0") apart, but ideally in wider rows that you can walk between. The drawback to seedling beds is of course that one is continually planting and replanting young delphiniums, which could lead to soil tiredness and other problems. Therefore the site should be varied as much as possible. One simple way to do this is to grow them in kitchen garden areas, rotating with vegetables and other flowers, or devise a scheme in which seedling beds are alternated with others containing, for example, annual bedding plants. Another possible approach used by some growers is to rent an allotment.

Many people do not have large gardens so that you might consider the alternative of growing seedlings in large pots, in order to see at least that the florets are of acceptable standard, only planting out those that are good and disposing of the remainder.

Once you have planted your young delphiniums, you will want to turn them into big ones as soon as possible. The key to doing so is by providing good cultivation.

There are two basic approaches to growing plants on. The first is one that has been followed by the majority of growers for many years. This traditional method aims to obtain large, fully mature delphiniums that flower in June or July of the year following planting. To achieve this, emphasis is placed on preventing them from flowering in the first year by a process known as disbudding or stopping. Shoots are allowed to develop up to the point that embryo flower spikes, what we call 'brushes' start to develop. Those are then pinched out, after which the flower stems will start to die back. They should be removed as new growth develops from the bases of the plants. The process is repeated as necessary, during the summer, and should redirect the plant's energies from the production of flowers to the development of a substantial root system and crown. This approach is tried and tested. It may be preferred to the more modern method, outlined below, if your plants tend to be weak growing and spindly, possibly because of a difficult and hungry soil type.

Some very experienced growers now believe, and have demonstrated in practice, that if good cultivation is given, the process of disbudding is unnecessary for delphiniums grown from seed. Provided that your soil is well prepared, that sensible amounts of balanced or high potash type fertilisers are given and that regular and conscientious watering is carried out; seed sown in March can produce substantial plants that are in flower six months later. Some thought is also being given to whether delphiniums from cuttings can be grown on in the same way but, so far, no firm conclusions have been drawn.

Neither of these two basic approaches, to growing delphiniums on, is wrong. The one that you follow is a matter of choice. Our recommendation is that, if you are growing plants from seed, then the more modern procedure should certainly be tried since it is simpler and less labour intensive.

Thinning

Mature delphiniums produce a considerable number of shoots, each spring. Some, such as 'Emily Hawkins' and 'Bruce', produce an awful lot. Generally speaking, those shoots will require thinning. If that is not done, then the plant will carry many small, poorly formed flowering spikes, on weak stems that will be prone to breakage and collapse. Therefore, it is recommended that the thinnest shoots should be removed in the spring. They can then be used as cuttings, which can be rooted to make new plants. We suggest that on small, or weak growing, plants the total shoots remaining should be reduced to a maximum of three. In the case of older, vigorous, plants the shoots should be reduced to between five or seven.

Staking

The best method of staking delphiniums is to use three canes of 1.2 mtrs (4'0") in length, placed around each plant, arranged in a triangle, and splayed outwards slightly toward their tops. Approximately 0.3 mtrs (1'0") of each cane should be inserted into the ground. In the case of very tall, for example 1.8 mtrs (6'0") plants, then 1.5 mtrs (5'0") canes would be better. As the plants grow, twine should be tied around the stakes so as to form a cage. It is important that individual stems should not be tied tightly beneath each spike, since this will create a point at which excessive stress will be created. This would cause stems to break, rather than prevent it. It is better, by far, to allow stems some freedom to sway within the cage already described.

It is a temptation to re-use older canes to stake delphiniums, in order to minimise costs. However, we do not recommend this since, in our experience, they break! It is better to buy new canes each year.

It is particularly important that staking should be carried out at an early stage, before stems become damaged or weakened by adverse weather. When working in and around delphinium plants you should always be very aware of the canes, for safety reasons, and their position in relation to your eyes. You can obtain brightly coloured rubber caps from nurseries and hardware shops that fit on the end of canes. Or, if you like a tipple, you can use corks from your empty wine bottles. Spectacles or eye protectors will also provide a safeguard against accidents.

There are a variety of purpose-made plant supports on the market. Those are expensive but can be very good. Examples are a half hoop with the ends bent to form legs, or stakes in which the top is bent to form a horizontal link to an adjoining one. We would suggest that plant supports should be considered for safety reasons, if you have plants that need support but are situated below a terrace or sloping ground, to prevent possible injury to elderly people or children falling into the flowerbed.

The objective of staking your plants is, of course, to keep them upright. You should also not ignore the need for shelter and should avoid planting delphiniums in especially windy positions if at all possible. For example, tall garden walls look as though they provide good shelter, but actually form solid obstructions to wind which causes air turbulence on their lee side; whereas hedges filter wind and allow a proportion of it to pass through, which is preferable. Similarly, surrounding trees provide good shelter from wind and the effects of weather generally, although delphiniums should not be planted underneath or very close to them.

Flowering and winter care

The normal flowering period for mature delphinium plants, in Britain, is between the latter part of June and the earlier part of July, although some exceptionally early or late flowering cultivars do extend the season somewhat.

When the delphinium stems attain about 1 mtrs (3'0") in height you will observe embryo 'brushes', which elongate and develop into substantial flower spikes, with many buds arranged in spirals around them. The buds, in turn, will develop into florets, the ones at the bottom opening first, with the buds at the top opening last.

When the main spikes set seed and drop their petals, they should be cut off just below their bases and removed, leaving the laterals (the flowering side shoots) to come into flower and so prolong the display. Those, in turn, should be cut off and removed after flowering.

Once the laterals have been removed, the remaining stems and foliage should be allowed to die back naturally. It is important to bear in mind that just because your plants have finished flowering and the top growth is dying back, they are not actually dead or dormant. They are in fact building up resources for over-wintering and then growing the following season. For those reasons it is important to ensure that they are well looked after, perhaps with an application of high potash or alternatively super-phosphate fertiliser and most certainly by ensuring that they are adequately watered.

Sometimes, it will be found that plants start to shoot strongly from the base, after they have flowered. In those cases, since the plant shows an inclination to have a second flowering later in the year, the older stems and leaves should be removed, without delay, to facilitate this.

Once the older stems and leaves have died back fully, by the autumn, we recommend that they should be cut off just above ground level and removed. The delphinium beds or borders then should be weeded, tidied and made ready for the winter. If you choose to protect delphinium crowns with coarse river sand, or some similar material, to deter slugs then early autumn is the time to renew it. Of course, regular precautions against slugs should be taken during the winter. It may be cold, but in our experience it is never too cold for them!

Fertilisers and manures

Natural fertilisers can be either compost or animal manure. Both provide valuable humus that can be added to the soil, improving texture, aeration and water retentiveness. It is important to stress that if you make your own compost, adding dead delphinium stems, crowns or roots to it is definitely not recommended because of the possibility of spreading virus, fungal or bacterial infections amongst your plants. Not all animal manures are alike and growers have their individual preferences. For one well-known enthusiast, the big thing was elephant dung. He would wait eagerly for the annual visit of the circus but, before we mock him, it must be said that he was a very successful exhibitor. However, it is not really necessary to go to such extremes. Horse manure is accepted generally as being the best type whilst cow manure is acceptable. Chicken manure, however, is very high in nitrogen and is not recommended because it will make plants grow very lush with abundant leaves, but rather at the expense of flowers and certainly with a reduction in weather resistance and perenniality. Incorporating manure or compost into the soil is highly beneficial. It improves both soil structure and water retentiveness. Manure should always be old, well rotted and well weathered before use, so that any possible contaminants will have been leached out. It is recommended that it should be applied in the autumn, taking care not to cover the dormant delphinium crowns since that could encourage rot or slugs.

Artificial fertilisers are also of different types. Some are high in nitrogen. Others are balanced formulations or contain high levels of potash and phosphates. An analysis of the constituents of fertilisers is usually given on the packets in which they are supplied. Balanced fertilisers should be used to feed delphiniums during the early part of the growing season. Alternatively, use the high potash/high phosphate types, and certainly do so at the end of the growing season. Whereas nitrogen encourages leaf and stem growth, potash encourages greater flower size as well as more intense colour. Phosphates encourage good, healthy root growth, which is vital if the delphinium plants are to be fully hardy and perennial.

Liquid fertilisers are also available. These, too, can be nitrogenous, balanced or high potash types. They are quick acting and can be used to perk up any plants that are growing poorly, but don't overdo it and ensure that you use the correct recommended dilutions. Remember that liquid fertiliser should be watered around but not onto plants, since it can 'burn' leaves and stems. 'Phostrogen' is a typical and recommendable high potash/high phosphate fertiliser, supplied in powder form that can be diluted.

Finally, there are 'foliar feeds'. These are sprayed onto the leaves of a plant and will tone it up nicely. In particular, the leaves will be a darker and richer green.

Watering

Conscientious and regular watering is at least as important as feeding. Delphiniums are large plants and are relatively shallow rooted. They need, therefore, a lot of water during the growing season. It is also most important to keep watering them after they have flowered, since this is when the eyes, or next year's buds, are formed on the crown. For a plant to grow, flower and then set seed is a very strenuous process, from which it needs to recover if it is to over-winter and flower well in the following season.

Weeding, hoeing and mulching

The importance of keeping flowerbeds free of weeds is not merely cosmetic. Weeds rob the soil of nutrients and also use up a lot of water that could otherwise be taken up by your delphiniums. They also act as a host for virus, eelworms and other soil pests. Regular, shallow, hoeing between your plants will help to keep the ground weed free. It will also keep the top inch of soil broken up, which will in turn reduce evaporation of water from the soil during hot periods. It is important to bear in mind that delphinium roots lie close to the surface of the soil. Therefore, do not hoe too deeply.

Similar objectives to hoeing can be achieved by mulching, that is to say by adding a layer of organic material on to the soil surface. If the mulch is not well rotted, the biological process of decay will rob the soil beneath of nitrogen, which is an essential plant nutrient. A wide variety of materials can be used that include shredded bark or compost. Permeable plastic sheets can be used but contain no nutrients. Their function is primarily weed suppression and water conservation. Spent mushroom compost also contains very few nutrients but delphiniums respond well to its use as a mulch.

It is recommended that mulches should be applied in the spring, taking care that this is done when the soil is wet, rather than dry.

Growing in containers and under glass

Plants raised for decorating The Delphinium Society's stand at the Chelsea Flower Show are grown in pots, which are placed under glasshouse protection early in the year. These delphiniums, which are the Society's showcase, require a good deal of care and attention with regard to watering, feeding, thinning and staking. But the end product shows that they will quite happily put on a good display in pots if a certain amount of care is taken.

Why not try half a dozen pots for your patio? The method is to select cuttings, which have broken from the base, and place them in two or three litre pots. At the same time a cane is inserted alongside the growing point. Compost is a matter of personal choice but John Innes number three mixed with mushroom compost in the proportion of roughly two thirds to one third will give satisfactory results. As the plants grow they will regularly need to be checked for water. When the root system is well developed but before becoming root bound the plants should receive their final potting. Seven and a half litre size is recommended for this, using the same compost mixture as before. The final potting should take place by the end of August to enable the roots to take good hold of the new soil before the advent of cold weather. To avoid possible root damage the following year, when your plants will flower, three canes can be inserted in a triangle around the perimeter.

When growth has ceased, in the autumn, remove old leaves and stems. Then place the pots where they will be protected from the worst of the winter rains. They need no protection from winter frosts, but should be rested on battens so that excess moisture can run off freely. The usual precautions against slugs are also necessary.

Plants grown in pots do have a tendency to start growth earlier in the season than do those in the ground and it is quite likely that the first signs of life will appear in January. When growth is well and truly under way, it will be necessary to restrict the number of stems. The final aim is to reduce those to two or possibly three in the case of strongly growing plants. At about the beginning of March it is a good idea to scratch into the surface a tablespoonful of blood, fish and bone, and then to water in. After that, at weekly intervals, a watering with high potash fertiliser such as 'Phostrogen' is all that is required. Of course, watering is required as necessary, which as growth progresses will be almost daily. Please remember that our average rainfall is not sufficient. Plants will most probably be in bloom by the middle of June, by which time two ties around the already inserted canes will enable the flowers to sway in the breeze.

Delphiniums can be forced to flower early, for example in time for the Chelsea

Flower Show, which takes place in May. To achieve this, pots are placed under glass in early January and thereafter tended the same as if grown in containers outside, with one exception. The exception being that once started into growth they should not be frosted. Temperatures ideally should not drop below 4.5°C (40°F), the intention being to avoid any check in their growth. On sunny days in March plants can grow inches in a day. To prevent unduly tall spikes it is a good idea to place them outside in a warm spot and replace under cover early evening. Size of greenhouse, siting, amounts of sun or cloud can make such a difference that only by experimentation can experience be gained. Growing under glass and starting with two or three plants can be very rewarding and not especially time consuming. Imagine having your very own flower show while Chelsea is on!

The advantage of being 'mobile' is that you can place your delphiniums where they can be seen at their best, but also moved out of wind and rain as necessary. The disadvantage is the need for constant watering, especially in a hot or windy period. But it is really worth it. Do have a try.

Staking delphiniums: Delphiniums are best given support by three canes arranged in a triangle around the plant and splayed slightly outwards. Stems should not be tied directly to the canes. Winding twine around the canes forms a cage, to allow stems to sway.

Godinton Park: A delphinium bed at Godinton Park, Ashford. Its trustees have made these available for the Kent and East Sussex Group of the Delphinium Society to use. The cultivars are, from left to right, 'Pandora', 'Fenella', 'Sungleam', 'Celebration', 'Loch Leven' and Patricia Johnson.

7, Dunstarn Lane, Adel, Leeds: The garden of the Delphinium Society's late President, Richard Wainwright. Delphiniums have been grown in this garden since before the Society was founded. The top photograph shows the garden in 1971, when the planting at the rear of the borders was nothing but delphiniums. Latterly, more of a mixed border effect has been aimed for, as shown in the more recent photograph at the bottom of the page.

Gants Mill, Bruton, Somerset: Delphiniums are used as specimen plants, rather than massed for effect, forming part of an overall garden design scheme.

A Yorkshire garden: There is a massive planting of delphiniums at the back of the border, but with lower growing herbaceous plantings in front, to conceal the delphiniums once they have finished flowering and the foliage dies back.

'Sandpiper': Probably the most desirable white delphinium. It has a dark brown eye. It was raised and introduced by Roy Latty.

The Wisley Trials: Held annually at the Royal Horticultural Society garden in Surrey, where delphiniums are assessed for awards.

Delphiniums at Harlow Car: Seedlings in 1981, raised by the Delphinium Society, under a breeding programme, grown and maintained by a 'local group' but with and with the help and assistance of the Northern Horticultural Society. Harlow Car is now owned and administered by the R.H.S.

'Gillian Dallas': A fine plant, raised and introduced by the firm of Blackmore and Langdon. It is a good plant both for the general garden and for exhibition.

Exhibition spikes of 'Dora Larkan': Raised and introduced by Clive Rowe, who cross-pollinated 'Skyline' x 'Loch Nevis'.

'Staking delphiniums'

Godinton Park

7 Dunstarn Lane, Adel, Leeds (1971)

7 Dunstarn Lane, Adel, Leeds (2001)

Gants Mill, Bruton, Somerset

A Yorkshire garden

'Sandpiper'

The Wisley Trials

Delphiniums at Harlow Car (1981)

'Gillian Dallas'

Exhibition spikes of 'Dora Larkan'

CHAPTER FIVE

EXHIBITING DELPHINIUMS

By Ray Joslyn

Unlike those who have a special interest in some other flowers, delphinium growers can take part in exhibiting, without the need to protect the blooms during their development. We can all therefore still enjoy the displays in our gardens in addition to comparing the best of the spikes or florets with those of fellow competitors, whether they be Delphinium Society members or within a local horticultural unit. Not least, we have the opportunity to advertise the merits of growing delphiniums to the general public and there is no better way to do this.

If any plant is worth growing it is worth growing well. With that in mind, everyone can become an exhibitor if they feel so inclined. There are many advantages apart from the competition itself. Among these are the social aspects of comparing views and ideas as to the best cultivars to grow and the various techniques adopted to obtain maximum results. Whilst it is always satisfying to win prizes, it is the taking part that really is enjoyable and well worth the extra effort of growing plants that are worthy of being included in a show.

Unless one is totally dedicated to growing delphiniums for the sole purpose of exhibiting, there is no advantage in growing exclusively those cultivars which are potential prize winners. There are a large number that are attractive garden plants which are unlikely to do well at shows, but a great deal of pleasure is lost if such cultivars are excluded from a collection. There is some advantage in growing delphiniums among other herbaceous plants, for an impressive garden display, although more particular attention can be given to individual plants if a separate bed is provided for show quality spikes.

Once it has been established which are the best cultivars to grow for exhibiting purposes, one has a distinct advantage over those who are embarking on showing other types of flower. This is because of the limited number of delphiniums that are suited to exhibition standards. It is usual to see several of the same cultivar in each class, whereas in other specialist flower shows it is sometimes only those exhibitors who are prepared to build up a collection of the best, and sometimes the most expensive, that can compete successfully. In this respect, delphinium growers all start with an equal opportunity should they wish to become exhibitors, always assuming they possess a good basic collection of named cultivars. It is worth emphasising here that only those cultivars that originate from specialist growers should be considered for exhibition purposes as it is extremely unlikely that garden centres will stock the best elatum hybrids.

Exhibitors manage to succeed regardless of growing in a variety of soil types although those having heavy clay are at a disadvantage, as are those growing in similar ground for general garden display. If, however, the clay can be broken up sufficiently to enable grit to be incorporated, or any other means of creating a less compact medium can be achieved, then delphiniums will grow satisfactorily. A good soil texture containing suitable quantities of humus is necessary for the cultivation of any herbaceous plant left in the same position for several years and this applies particularly to delphiniums.

There is no special formula for the feeding of show quality plants but obtaining a professional soil test before applying fertilisers is to be recommended; although it is not essential if plant growth is known to be good. An early season, high nitrogen, feed helps to boost the structure of plant growth. A later emphasis on potash will provide a ripening of the stems and promote good flower quality, but feeding should not be overdone at any stage, otherwise distortion and gappy flower formation will result. Limited experimenting with feeding programmes is the best way to establish what best suits your delphiniums. One treatment which should be applied whatever the soil conditions is a good layer of mulching early in the season, preferably whilst the soil is moist from winter rain and after the early application of feed.

In order to obtain good quality flower spikes for exhibiting it is recommended that the early growth should be thinned, either by removing the shoots for propagation or discarding the weakest. It is obviously better to do this gradually so that the strongest shoot growth is reduced to three or four per plant, plus one spare as a safeguard against any later damage. The precise number to keep depends on the particular cultivar and only by observation can it be decided which are vigorous enough to enable more shoots to be retained. In some cases only two or three emerge, which might reflect the limited vigour of the plant or a decline in its health. The important thing is to grow on the strongest for exhibition purposes and give them extra care until the time comes to decide which are at the best and in their prime for the show date.

Once having decided to make entries in a show, it is first necessary to check the schedule of classes to ascertain which of your cultivars can be included. Depending on the weather conditions at the time of submitting an entry form, an estimate has to be made as to the expected stage of each plant's development on the show date. No attempt should be made to include those that are showing their seed pods or dropping petals. As a general rule, a spike having at least two thirds of its florets open at the time of cutting should be at the right stage of development when being judged. However, there are no hard and fast views on this since much depends on the cultivar concerned, the time of day when cut and the temperature.

Care should be taken when deciding on the cultivars to be included in a show entry, particularly where the schedule calls for spikes with blue or perhaps light or dark coloured florets. The Delphinium Society publishes a list of plants that are acceptable in those categories from time to time. However, it is unlikely that, in local horticultural societies, such restrictions in their delphinium classes would occur.

The best time for cutting spikes for a show depends on the prevailing weather conditions. A decision must also be made according to the exhibitor's available time. A cool garage area or similar should be used (any time from the morning of the day before the show would be appropriate) to store the cut spikes. It is important to place those in containers of water, for a few hours before transporting to the show. The period must depend on the time to be spent travelling in what can often be very hot conditions in a vehicle.

The equipment needed before starting the cutting, and during the preparation which includes staging, should include a sharp knife or small toothed saw, containers of sufficient size to accommodate the cut spikes, a small watering can, material for packing stems in the vases, cotton wool, copy of the show schedule. Also, of course, a vehicle of suitable length for transporting (it is essential, having cut each spike, to ensure that they will fit in the space available).

It is advisable to cut each spike at an angle, initially with about 380mm (15") of stem and then carry with care to a preparation area away from any strong winds. After removing all the large leaves and carefully cutting off lateral growths, the spike needs to be held upside down to enable water to be poured into the stem. To do this without causing an airlock, keep the inverted spike slightly off the vertical position whilst filling with a small watering can. Once charged with water the spike is in need of support at the next stage when, having placed a thumb over the open end (or plugged with cotton wool if preferred), bring the spike back to its upright position and place in a previously filled container. Keep the thumb in place until the stem is immersed, if using this method.

Various ways of transporting the selected show spikes can be used, either in long boxes with soft linings of tissue paper on crumpled newspaper, or simply the same lining material placed in the vehicle. It will be necessary to refill or top up the stems before transporting but this time a firmly placed plug of cotton wool must be used to avoid leakages whilst in transit. As well as the equipment already mentioned it is important to pick enough unblemished leaves for dressing the vases when staging. It is better to keep those in water until commencing your journey, and then in a plastic bag until required.

When arriving at the show venue, first check that a suitable space is available and then collect enough vases charged with water before unloading your delphiniums. Calculate how much of the bottom stem is to be retained, to enable a clear 100mm (4") to be visible between the top of the vase and lower florets before finally trimming to size. After that, refill each spike with water (a longer length of exposed stem can be left if there is a danger of damaging florets with lengthy pedicels). The same methods of placing in water can be adopted as described when first cutting, but it is essential now that the stems are completely filled when they are staged. Otherwise, flagging of the spikes will occur. Whatever is used for packing around each stem, it must be done firmly with space made to receive leaf stems for final dressing around the top of each vase. All then that remains to be done, once the vases are in their respective class positions, is to place entry cards with each exhibit, together with cards for stating the name of cultivar.

There are usually classes for displayed florets at delphinium shows and also at some of the local horticultural events. This involves the individual florets being removed from a selected spike with a sufficient length of pedicel to enable whatever number of florets are specified to be staged in water. Usually a wire netting covered bowl is provided which should be dressed with delphinium leaves to create a decorative effect. The advantage of exhibiting florets only is that the main spike need not be removed and taking off the required number of bottom florets does not spoil the garden display very much.

These notes are intended as a guide for first time exhibitors and with a little experience most people will adopt their own methods. Whether an interest is developed for exhibiting depends on a desire to share our achievements; it is not a matter of "pot hunting" for awards. It is quite surprising how much knowledge is gained when meeting fellow enthusiasts at shows and those delphiniums in our gardens can benefit from indulging ourselves in this way.

Judging criteria

Having grown our delphiniums well and transported and staged them to the best of our ability; it is up to the show judges to decide upon the degree of success we have achieved. The following guidelines for judges and exhibitors has been compiled by The Delphinium Society:

Exhibited Spikes

These should be long, tapering or columnar in shape with at least two thirds of florets open. Staged with a minimum 100mm (4") of stem visible below the bottom florets. Preferably with no laterals attached

Florets should be of good substance and colour, whether of self, contrasting colour or striped, showing even placement. Well-furnished florets of circular outline, with neat and even eye petals are preferred.

Presentation is important, with staging carried out to present an upright spike with clean foliage inserted around it to conceal packing. Spikes that are underdeveloped, crooked or malformed should be disregarded or severely down pointed, as should those with stripped florets or conspicuous seed pods.

Down pointing should also apply where spikes are sparsely or irregularly furnished with florets, or overcrowded.

Pointing:	Condition	5 points
	Form and size of spike	5 points
	Florets	5 points
	Overall effect	5 points
	Total	20 points
	Uniformity (for multiple spike classes)	3 points

As can be seen from the above, 25% of total points for exhibited spikes are shared between form and size. Therefore, size should not be at the expense of form. Getting the right balance between these two requirements is a result of an adequate, but not excessive feeding programme.

Vases of laterals

Stems should be well furnished with florets, evenly spaced, of good colour and the stems to be of sufficient substance to carry the weight of the florets.

Displayed Florets

These should be of the quality described above, eveness and careful matching being of added importance when florets are displayed.

Pointing:	Condition	5 points
	Substance and clearness of colour	5 points
	Size and uniformity	5 points
	Presentation	5 points
	Total	20 points

CHAPTER SIX

PESTS & DISEASES

By Patrick Booth

Delphiniums are affected, like other plants, by a range of pests and diseases but most are relatively uncommon or easily dealt with. The purpose of this book is to give very comprehensive information, so that if you do have a problem, you can find out what it is and how to deal with it. The existence of so many pests and diseases within the covers of a book does not mean that they are all out in the garden, devastating your plants. Many will not be encountered in many years of growing delphiniums. The main problem is that if you want to grow delphiniums successfully, you must deal with slugs and snails and be ruthless in order to achieve success. Delphiniums are not alone in being eaten since many other plants are attacked. Killing and deterring slugs and snails really is an essential task, not just for specialist delphinium growers but also for gardeners in general.

Fortunately, as already explained, other problems are relatively uncommon. You are far more likely to have to deal with general garden pests, for example moles, than by all of the more unusual delphinium ailments put together. However, in the longer term it is advisable to take sensible precautions against soil tiredness and the build up of parasitic eelworms, by adopting crop rotation principles.

For many years, amateur gardeners have had access to a veritable arsenal of potions and powders, designed to wreak havoc on pests and diseases. There has been a gradual change from some of the more extreme pest controls such as 'Paris Green', a preparation that used to be recommended as a slug killer and which was based on arsenic.

An EEC licensing system for pesticides and fertilisers has now been introduced. Our choice will be restricted, for the foreseeable future, since the costs of obtaining approval by manufacturers is high in relation to the potential profit to be made from products intended for use by amateur gardeners. The problem is compounded because the use of agricultural chemicals by amateur gardeners is illegal. Whilst the general aims of checking, for safety reasons, should be applauded, the bureaucracy is a major concern since gardeners are deprived of perfectly safe remedies because of cost.

A number of well-known gardening products appear to have been discontinued whilst others have been re-branded. The result is that there is quite a lot of confusion, which is likely to continue for some time. For that reason we may refer to trade names within this book, but may also include the active ingredients that are usually shown on product labels so that substitutes can be identified. The consequence of the reduction in the number of pesticides and chemical solutions, available to amateur gardeners, will probably be that many of us will have to go 'back to school' and start brushing up on organic gardening methods. We will have to think, also, more about taking precautions to avoid pests and diseases than in seeking remedies for them. For those reasons, we place a lot of emphasis on crop rotation principles; to avoid soil based problems or diseases. We also emphasise the need for good garden hygiene.

Slugs & snails

Slugs and snails are the most serious pests to afflict delphiniums. They eat the eyes and shoots, which in itself is bad enough since they always go for the fattest, juiciest ones, which means that the quality of the flowers grown suffers. Not so noticeable but equally seriously the wounds left on the crown provide a route by which a plant can be invaded by fungi, bacteria and any eelworms that may be present in the surrounding soil. Many gardeners are discouraged from growing the plants because they have so many slugs and snails in their garden. This is a pity since the problem is not normally insurmountable. There are four basic ways in which slugs and snails can be controlled, those are:

1. Collection methods.
2. Chemical control.
3. Using deterrents.
4. Biological measures.

The merits of these different approaches are discussed below. It is up to you however, to decide which ones are most suitable for yourself.

Collection methods

Slugs and snails will be more of a problem on heavy, wet soils than on light sandy ones. Whatever the soil, good garden hygiene helps. This should include keeping the garden weed free and making sure that there is no rubbish under which slugs like to shelter. For those with strong stomachs, environmentally friendly 'slug hunts' can be carried out on wet evenings by torchlight, hand picking the pests and drowning them in a bucket of salty water.

Provided that the garden is generally free of weeds and rubbish then shelter, such as tiles or inverted grapefruit segments, can be provided for slugs and snails in strategic places that they will hide underneath. They can then be collected and disposed of conveniently during the day.

Snails can be present on the leaves and stems of delphiniums. The best way of dealing with them is by hand picking.

Chemical control

The most effective method of controlling slugs and snails is by using pellets that contain either metaldehyde or methiocarb as the active ingredients. We think that the methiocarb pellets are no longer available for amateur gardeners in Britain at the present time. Metaldehyde pellets, which are readily available, are slightly less effective and a lot cheaper. We believe also that they pose a smaller threat to animals and wildlife. Many people are concerned that birds, including thrushes, eat poisoned slugs and die as a result. However, we believe that there is no firm evidence for or against this theory. Populations of some bird species have certainly reduced in Britain, but many things could have caused this. Those include intensive farming methods, with reductions in the number of hedges, and also the activities of domestic cats and other predators such as birds of prey.

We believe that the risks associated with pellets are greatly exaggerated. They are nowadays treated with 'bitrex' or similar substances that deter animals and birds, and also with a blue colouring that appears unnatural. Pellets, under current EEC regulations, must contain a maximum of 3% metaldehyde. Therefore, if they are distributed thinly over the soil and in accordance with the manufacturer's recommendations, rather than in small piles, the possibility of harming animals and birds will be minimised. You should apply pellets regularly to get maximum effect.

Whether to use slug pellets is of course a matter of choice. If you are opposed to using them, in any shape or form, there are liquid preparations, based on either metaldehyde or aluminium sulphate, that can be used.

A major advantage in using aluminium sulphate based preparations is that they will destroy the eggs of slugs and snails. During the winter a solution, that has been diluted in accordance with the manufacturer's instructions, may be applied two or three times to the dormant plants and surrounding soil. A double strength dose can be used on compost heaps, around the bases of walls and other locations where slugs are likely to shelter, but should not be used around your prized plants.

Aluminium sulphate is slightly caustic, so that you should avoid watering directly onto plants during the growing season, as this would burn leaves and stems. An additional problem with aluminium sulphate preparations is that they act as soil acidifiers. If you have acid soil, then the treatment should be followed by an application of lime in the spring, or alternatively by mulching with mushroom compost, which contains lime.

'Beer traps' or 'slug pubs' are containers designed to hold beer, to which slugs are attracted, fall into the liquid, become intoxicated and then drown. Many growers have reported that these devices work, to some extent but are not a complete solution. We would suggest that you use strong beer, alcohol by volume (ABV) 4.5 or stronger, and replace it every two to three days.

Deterrents

Slugs and snails do not like to cross sharp, abrasive and dry materials; a traditional precaution is to place such things as grit, coarse (not fine builders) sand, soot or crushed eggshells around plants. It is important however to ensure that the materials used are open in texture so that they dry quickly and do not form a hard shell or cap that would prevent young emerging shoots from penetrating.

Biological methods

There is a modern method of destroying slugs, in the shape of nematodes. These are microscopic animals (phasmarhbditis hermaphrodita) that are parasitical, attacking and killing slugs. The mantles of affected slugs become enlarged after two or three days and they die below ground in about five.

Nematodes can be purchased from specialist companies in small bags, the contents of which are diluted in accordance with the manufacturer's instructions, then watered onto and around plants. They are effective but, unfortunately, only in a limited way. Drawbacks include cost. The treatment only protects for six weeks and it does not kill snails. Finally, the treatment only works when temperatures are greater than 5°C (41°F) so that it is ineffective during the winter.

Hedgehogs are a natural predator of slugs and snails. They can eat a great number of the pests every night and can be attracted by providing winter shelter (for example piles of leaves) and a little (not too much or foxes, badgers and rats may be attracted) tinned cat or dog meat. Do not feed on bread and milk since that is harmful to them. Hedgehogs are omnivorous. Many people worry that they could be killed, by eating slug pellets. Therefore, if your chosen approach is to encourage them, you may wish to consider avoiding the use of slug pellets and use liquid preparations instead. Of course, the snag with hedgehogs is that just when you want them to get really busy eating up all the slugs, in the winter with no need on your part to go outside, they are all hibernating!

Fasciation

Fasciation is a term used to describe a malformation of the delphiniums flower spike or stems, which may be curled or crooked, bunched, or flattened. The cause can be some abnormality in the weather, during the early growing season, overfeeding, over-thinning or spray drift from weed-killer. Usually, it is a temporary problem that should correct itself in the next growing season. However, some delphiniums are affected more than other ones. Therefore, if a particular plant is affected every year, it may be better to discard it.

Virus

Cucumber mosaic virus can occasionally affect delphiniums. The symptoms are that the leaves acquire a marbled discoloration and become elongated. The plants affected in this way are unsightly and weak growing. They do not recover from the effects of virus, which can be spread by insects such as aphids, and also by some nematodes (eelworm) which live in the soil. The only solution to virus infection is the drastic one of digging the plant up and burning, not composting, it.

Weeds can act as hosts for virus diseases. Chickweed, for example, is almost always infected with cucumber mosaic even though there are few visible signs. Therefore regular weeding is important.

Other viruses can affect delphiniums but are, happily, rare. Symptoms are usually some form of severe malformation of individual flowers or leaves. Be careful, however, that you do not confuse those with fasciation, or other physiological problems, which are more common and from which plants will recover. If more than one plant is affected, then the problem is unlikely to be virus.

Caterpillars and insects

Golden Plusia moth caterpillars feed mostly on monkshoods and delphiniums. Some others such as the angleshade and the cabbage moth also sometimes feed on delphiniums. Careful checks of plants should be made just as embryo flower spikes are forming in the early summer. It will be found occasionally that leaves are stuck to the sides with a caterpillar, which can be hand picked and disposed of, nestling within.

Delphiniums are not normally infested by aphids, but are visited from time to time. This is not a major problem, except that viruses can be spread, for which reason particular hosts such as Roses in the neighbourhood should be kept free of infestation.

Delphiniums can be affected by leaf miners, the larvae of a small fly (*phytomyza aconita*), living in small colonies within the foliage. Symptoms are small, whitish green spots. The pest is not common or serious and can be treated by using systemic insecticides.

Mildew & fungus diseases

Most gardeners are familiar with mildew, a powdery white fungus that affects roses in particular, but is by no means confined to them. A considerable number of ornamental plants are also affected, including some delphiniums, usually those with purple or mauve florets. Powdery mildew can become a real problem, and can seriously weaken delphinium plants if they are allowed to dry out in hot weather. It is vital that the plants should be kept well watered.

Delphiniums can also be affected by other fungal infections, which may also contribute to crown rot. Fortunately, there are a considerable number of fungicides available, many of which are systemic in action. That is to say that the active ingredients penetrate the plant as a whole. We suggest that you should spray all your plants with systemic fungicide before and after flowering, as a precaution.

Black leaf spot or black blotch

Black leaf spot, otherwise known as black blotch, is caused by bacteria (*Pseudomonas syringae* pv. *Delphinae*) that live in the soil and which can be spread by rain splash. Symptoms are black blotches that are formed on the leaves, stems and even, sometimes, the flower buds. The best control is by means of using liquid copper fungicide, which is also effective against soil bacteria, sprayed onto the affected plants.

Soil tiredness

It is well known that growing any plant continuously in the same ground, for many years will result in the soil becoming tired. This is the reason that, in medieval times, farmers allowed their fields to lie fallow. Modern agriculture involves the principle of crop rotation. Soil tiredness is caused by depletion of specific trace elements that particular plants need, coupled with a cumulative build up of minor pests and diseases that, together result in a serious drop in vigour.

We think that the best way for amateur growers to deal with the problem is to avoid it in the first place; by means of self-restraint and avoiding over-cultivation, using crop rotation principles rather than growing the delphiniums in every available space. Sensible principles of good husbandry and garden hygiene should also help, whilst the soil can be revitalised by manuring and enrichment.

Eelworms

Eelworms, which are types of nematode, are small nearly microscopic creatures that live in the soil as well as plants. Delphiniums are not commonly affected but some infestations do occur from root lesion eelworm or leaf and bud eelworm. There are some others, such as the stem eelworm that commonly affects phlox, which may also affect delphiniums. Other eelworms do not appear to affect delphiniums directly but are suspected of spreading viruses.

Root lesion eelworm

Delphiniums can be affected by root lesion eelworms (*Pratylenchus* Spp.). They live in the soil and invade the root systems of susceptible plants, feeding and breeding within them, destroying the fine roots and eventually leading to the weakening and rot of the crown followed by collapse of the whole plant.

Root lesion eeelworms are commonly present in soils but not, usually, in large quantities. However, the monoculture of susceptible plants coupled with poor cultivation practices and garden hygiene can cause a gradual build up of infestation over a period of years, eventually leading to severe problems. Rather than waiting for infestations to develop, it is sensible to take precautions that, similar to avoiding soil tiredness, involve principles of crop rotation. You should take care to avoid other susceptible plants in your planting scheme, such as other members of the Ranunculaceae family, including hellebores, larkspurs, clematis, thalictrum and aconitum, but also other known targets such as bulbous lilies and narcissus.

The build up of root lesion eelworm populations, in the soil, is normally slow on uncultivated ground. However digging, hoeing and in particular rotovating will spread infestations more quickly. If substantial infestations build up in the soil, plants grown in it will cease to thrive. Yellowing and wilting stems and leaves will become evident, leading to collapse of the plants together with rotting of their crowns and roots. As soon as it becomes apparent that plants are affected in this way, they should be carefully dug up, with surrounding root ball, and disposed of.

Large nurseries may relocate their delphinium fields from time to time, to avoid problems arising from soil tiredness and, in particular, eelworm infestation. They also have access to soil sterilisation procedures that are not available to amateur growers and which are difficult to apply.

It needs to be emphasised that root lesion eelworm infestation of delphiniums is a long-term problem and one that very few amateur growers ever experience. But if you think that your soil is affected you should take samples and have them tested. You should be aware that if the results are positive, there are no effective chemical treatments available to amateur growers. However, research has shown that French and African marigolds (tagetes) have root secretions that reduce eelworm populations in the soil to a very substantial extent, provided that they are grown in it for a minimum of three or four months. If that possible solution doesn't work, then the simplest course of action is to start afresh in a different part of the garden, with completely new plants.

Leaf and bud eelworm

Otherwise called the chrysanthemum eelworm (*Aphenchoides* Spp.) infest the leaves and stems of susceptible plants which include, in addition to delphiniums; chrysanthemums, dahlias, phlox, paeonies, calcaeolarias, doronicums, lavenders, penstemons, pyrethrums, rudbeckias, verbenas, wallflowers, zinnias and buddleia.

Symptoms are black or brown discoloration on leaves and stems where the tissues have been killed. These are usually limited in area by thicker leaf veins so that they appear irregular. The infestations pass up the plants and can be spread by rain splash. The soil may be affected as a result but the eelworm will not survive in it for long. They may live for up to 3 months, however, in dead plant tissues.

Affected plants are best dug up and disposed of. As usual, it is best to take precautions. In this respect, you should understand that the most likely sources of infection are plants imported into your garden from elsewhere. It therefore follows that any new plants, for the garden, should be obtained only from reputable nurserymen and that they should be checked carefully for evidence of disease before planting.

Crown and root rots

Rotting of delphinium crowns is usually not the result of eelworm infestation. It can and does occur most commonly as a result of various bacterial and fungal infections, resulting either from excessively wet ground, damage by slugs and snails or else because of the old age of the plant. Crown rot usually occurs during the winter, but may also happen occasionally during the growing season.

Diseases of delphinium crowns and roots fall into two basic categories. The first is associated with fungal attacks entering via the root system. The second category is associated with bacterial soft rot that affects the crown directly. To guard against these particular diseases, you should cultivate your plants to a good standard and avoid excessive use of highly nitrogenous fertilisers, which soften delphinium crowns. You should also take scrupulous precautions against slugs and snails, which by attacking the crown and young shoots leave wounds that ease the path of fungal and bacterial diseases.

Generally speaking, bacterial decay has traditionally been regarded as a more serious problem than fungal rot, because it does not respond to soil sterilisation. However, since soil sterilisation is not normally an option for amateur gardeners, plants affected by any form of root or crown rot should be dealt with in the same way. If a delphinium dies, as they do from time to time, whether as a result of old age, crown or root rot, it should be dug up with surrounding root ball and disposed off, but do not simply replace it with another delphinium in the same position. We suggest that you soak the ground, as a precaution, with something like 'Jeyes Fluid' or 'Armillatox'. Then after two or three weeks plant something else.

Pests and diseases in North America

Britain is a small country. Because of this, pests and diseases will be very much the same, wherever you are. In North America the size of the continent is such that the types, which affect plants, will vary greatly. Generally speaking, the range of diseases that attack delphiniums, will be similar to those in Britain but there are also some others that affect plants in North America and other parts of the world (but not Britain). The most important of those are listed below.

Black Rot

Delphiniums in Britain are not affected by true 'Black Rot' disease, which is caused by a fungus ('*Athelia Rolfsii*', also known as '*Sclerotium Rolfsii*' or '*Sclerotium Delphinii*'), confined to tropical, semi-tropical and warm temperate regions of the world. It is widespread within those areas and also has an enormous variety of host plants. Therefore, although Black Rot is particularly associated with North America, it must affect delphiniums in many other countries.

Sub-zero temperatures will kill the fungus. For example, although it has been recorded in Britain, it was unable to survive the winter. Although it can occur in all parts of North America it will only persist, from year to year, in the warmer and more humid areas. It will not survive the low winter temperatures of the northern states.

The first indications of infection are thin white threads (technically known as hyphae) that surround the bases of stems just above and below soil level. Small yellow and reddish brown bodies (sclerotia) then develop in the tangle of white threads and are about the size of large seeds. The fungus attacks the bases of the plant's stems. The initial symptoms will be accompanied by the rapid yellowing and collapse of the top growth followed by rotting of the crown. A dark reddish stain may remain on the surrounding soil.

The difference between ordinary crown and root rots and black rot is the ability of the latter to spread to other plants by means of the thread like hyphae. Therefore, in geographical areas where plants are at risk of this disease, it is imperative that a careful watch should be made for early symptoms. Any affected plants should be dug up quickly, with surrounding root ball, and disposed of or destroyed, without delay. They should, in no circumstances, be added to compost heaps.

The fungus that causes black rot does not, normally, spread by means of airborne spores, Its hyphae spread from infected plants. Therefore, the most likely cause of infestation is new plants imported into the garden. It is particularly important that those, and the compost, in which they are planted, should be checked. As a counsel of perfection we would suggest quarantining any new plants for at least a month, before they are put out into the garden. The fungus can attack a huge range of host plants so that no exceptions should be made.

Aster yellows disease

Delphiniums in Britain are not affected by Aster yellows disease, which is a significant problem in some parts of North America and Canada and is caused by a virus like organism called a phytoplasma.

Aster yellows disease is transmitted mainly by the aster (or six-spotted) leafhopper. These leafhoppers originate in the American mid-west and the south, migrating with the prevailing winds during the summer months. They act as a vector, transmitting the disease from infected plants.

Symptoms include yellowing of the foliage, the plants will come late into flower and the flowers will be green and distorted. As with virus diseases, there is no cure. Affected plants should be dug up and destroyed. Plants may be sprayed with suitable systemic insecticides as a precaution.

Cyclamen mite

Delphiniums in some parts of America can become infested with mites that are small, spider like creatures, requiring a magnifying glass to be seen. The most common of these are cyclamen mites, which cause badly distorted, thick and brittle foliage and flowers, with dark brown or black streaks and blotches.

Cyclamen mites overwinter in the dormant crowns of delphiniums. During the summer, they are most commonly found on immature leaves and buds. Delphinium plants, in areas prone to infestation, should be spaced apart so that their leaves do not touch. This will limit the spread of mites from plant to plant. The other main method of control is to spray regularly with a suitable insecticide.

CREATING FLORAL ART WITH DELPHINIUMS

By Anne Blissett

There have been many articles and books about flower arranging and although much time and preparation should go into the selection of colours, flower arranging is an expression of your own sense of beauty. Most people will have heard of Mrs. Constance Spry and her famous school. Her words still hold true ~ "Never forget that in arranging flowers you have an opportunity to express your own sense of what is beautiful and you should feel free and uninhibited in doing so". The main purpose of arranging flowers is to see that they are presented in the most satisfactory and effective way possible. You are creating a picture with your flowers, just as an artist does with a canvas and paint brush.

There are many suitable containers. If you love flowers in the home you will want to collect inspirational vases, dishes or bowls; an occasional exciting buy can still be made at a car boot or jumble sale! Care must be given to proportion and colour and there must be compatibility between the vase and flowers. The height of the container you use should be one-third to one-half the height of the tallest flowers and foliage you have picked. If the vase is more than this it will make them appear as if they are trying to peep out of the top – if it is less, then the arrangement will look as if it is about to topple over.

There are no hard and fast rules that must be slavishly obeyed, although there are a few basic guidelines that work for most flower arrangers; just remember the four design elements, which are form, texture, space and colour. Used with balance and proportion the resulting design will be harmonious and you will maximise the effect of the majestic delphiniums. As a general rule, try and cut them in the early morning or in the evening. During the day they will probably be moisture deficient and so more likely to droop as soon as they have been cut. When collecting flowers and foliage from the garden carry a bucket of water and immediately each stem is cut place it in the bucket. Always use a good pair of scissors or secateurs and make a clean cut at an angle, never tug at the plant or you may damage it. Blunt scissors will crush the stem and block it. The process of getting water up the stem as quickly as possible is known as 'conditioning'. Plants absorb moisture via their roots and once cut this flow is stopped. Conditioning restarts this and the sooner it is done the less opportunity there is for wilting. Tepid water is absorbed more quickly than cold and has a greater restorative value in the case of wilted flowers.

Delphiniums make a dramatic addition to the flower border and any arrangement of flowers. Pick the spikes when most of the florets are open. The lives of hollow-stemmed flowers, such as delphiniums, will be extended a little if immediately after cutting they are inverted and the stems filled with tepid water from a small can and plugged with cotton wool before being returned to the bucket. A thin cane may be gently inserted as far as you can up the stem if it is blocked. Once this is done, put out of direct sunlight to condition and leave overnight or through the day in deep water. If you cut flowers and foliage then arrange and put the container straight into the home, their life will be shortened by several days.

'Mechanics' are the means by which the flowers can be positioned exactly as required within the container, allowing everything to be shown to good advantage. They should never show, particularly in competitive work, whether they are floral foam, wire netting, pin-holders or any other aid. 'Wet' or 'Dry' floral foam may be purchased in block or cylinder form. 'Wet' foam intended for fresh flowers should be placed in deep water and will slowly sink as it absorbs moisture. It is easily cut to size and can now be obtained in many new colours – lime green, pink and yellow (which does not need to be hidden as it can complement an arrangement) in addition to the more usual dark green. 'Dry' foam is harder and is intended for preserved and silk flowers; it will not retain water. Wire netting, or chicken wire, can be used as a 'cap' over the foam giving extra support. Depending on the container, it can be crumpled into several thicknesses and used on its own as a support, or in conjunction with a pin-holder. To arrange delphiniums in a lovely glass vase, why not try glass marbles or coloured glass beads in similar colours – they hold the stems in place and are also decorative too!

For a large room, or particularly in a church, delphiniums are an ideal choice and are always remarked upon. They look magnificent arranged in pedestals, creating immediate impact because of their height and colours. When arranging delphiniums, or any other flowers, remember that no two spikes of the same length should be next to each other. Create an 'in and out' effect, rather than a flat level appearance and try to use odd numbers working in threes, fives, sevens, not squarely placed fours, sixes and eights. A good maxim to follow in designing floral arrangements is again one of Constance Spry's – "If in doubt, leave it out!" In recent years the following has also been added, "… and if its thin, bung it in!" Again, one of our more modern nationally acclaimed arrangers tells us not to pack more and more flowers into the arrangement, saying - "Don't forget to leave room for the butterflies!" Remember to add material to the back of the arrangement, which will obviously fall forward if all the spikes and foliage are to the front! Remove any leaves that will fall below the water line if using a vase – any leaves that touch the water will decay, clog up the stems and sour the water. It goes without saying that the water level should be checked daily.

It is difficult to give guidance on the type of foliage to use with delphiniums. Colour combinations depend on the variety of the delphinium used, but alchemilla mollis (Lady's Mantle) always looks good together with hellebores, euphorbias, cow parsley and other plants with lime and acid-green foliage.

In major delphinium shows and exhibitions, undoubtedly the large flowered, tall perennial hybrids are the 'stars of the show' and the laterals play a supporting role. However, within flower arranging circles, the laterals come into their own and are much coveted. Laterals are smaller, more versatile, easier to handle and tend to have a longer 'shelf life' than a full delphinium spike. Not to be discounted either are the small Belladonnas. A particular favourite for flower arrangers is a cultivar named 'Piccolo', a bright gentian blue that is free flowering and short growing.

When fresh flowers and foliage are scarce, attractive arrangements can be made with flowers, leaves and seed-heads, which have been dried. Delphiniums lend themselves to an air-drying process. Select well-formed spikes just before they are fully developed and pick on a dry day as this speeds dehydration and results in better colour retention. Remove the leaves because they shrivel and slow down the dehydration process.

Tie the stems firmly in small bunches taking care not to crush the florets. Hang them upside down so that the sap in the stems runs down and prevents the 'necks' from shrivelling before drying is completed. Leave until crisp to the touch but check the ties periodically as the stalks will shrink and the bunches could fall. Suitable places for hanging are in a dry garage or shed, with good air circulation and free from direct sunlight. Dried spikes should be stored carefully in a dry place as they are usually fragile. Cardboard boxes with lids prevent crushing – plastic bags are unsuitable as they hold condensation and encourage mildew. If the spikes are arranged with other dried material, the 'Dry' foam already mentioned should be used.

In 1959, flower arranging clubs and societies banded together and with the support of the Royal Horticultural Society, formed the National Association of Flower Arrangement Societies. Today, like the Delphinium Society, NAFAS ranks as one of the most notable specialist associations and is a world-wide fellowship. There are around 90,000 members within 1,400 affiliated clubs across 21 areas in the UK. There is probably one near you. NAFAS aims to encourage the love of flowers and plants, organises exhibitions and competitions, and instructs, trains and qualifies judges, demonstrators, speakers and teachers in order to raise the standard of floral art.

A delphinium floral arrangement: A very simple arrangement using alchemilla mollis (lady's mantle), variegated ivy and delphiniums.

Elatum delphinium showing roots, shoots and crown: Shoots grow upwards from the solid crown, whilst the roots grow downwards and outwards.

Cuttings must be taken at the junction of the shoots with the crown: The photograph shows a craft knife positioned correctly to slice off a cutting. If the cutting is taken too high, it will be hollow and will not root.

A comparison of cutting material: Cuttings should be solid and with no evidence of rot. The second cutting from the left is exceptionally clean. The cutting on the left is acceptable. Those on the right show some rot at their centre.

A water cutting: Dephinium cuttings can be rooted in a jar of water, with sharp sand or gravel in the bottom. There are variations used by professional nurserymen that allow larger quantities to be propagated.

Cuttings being rooted in perlite: Cuttings can, instead, be rooted in 'Perlite', stood in trays of water.

A rooted cutting: This cutting has been rooted in 'Perlite'. It is at about this stage in the plants development that the tip of the primary shoot should be disbudded, to encourage new shoots to break from the base.

'Loch Leven' in the walled garden at 'Temple Newsam': One advantage of being able to propagate your own delphiniums is that several of the same cultivar can be planted together, to increase their impact in the garden. 'Loch Leven, raised and introduced by Tom Cowan, is an excellent plant for the garden or exhibition.

Crown Jewel: This is an excellent delphinium raised and introduced by Blackmore and Langdon.

Taking eye-cuttings: As with conventional cuttings, these should be taken by cutting them off at the point where they join the crown.

A detached eye-cutting: Although there is rot in the base of the stem, the cutting taken from it is very clean and should root readily.

Eye-cuttings: The eye-cuttings are inserted into trays of sharp sand or other rooting medium. The tips of those shown are starting to 'green up', which is an indication hat rooting is taking place.

Rooted eye-cutting: Showing early root development.

'Walton Gemstone': An excellent delphinium, raised and introduced by Henry Wilkins.

'Chelsea Star': Raised and introduced by Blackmore and Langdon, its very bright purple colour is unsurpassed.

A delphinium floral arrangement

Elatum Delphinium showing roots, shoots and crown

Cuttings must be taken at the junction of the shoots with the crown

A comparison of cutting material

Water cuttings

Cuttings being rooted in 'Perlite'

A rooted cutting

'Loch Leven' in the walled garden at 'Temple Newsam'

'Crown Jewel'

Taking eye-cuttings

A detached eye-cutting

Eye-cuttings

Rooted eye-cutting

'Walton Gemstone'

'Chelsea Star'

CHAPTER EIGHT

PROPAGATION

By Patrick Booth

Why would we want to propagate delphiniums from cuttings, eye cuttings or division, when some seed strains are claimed to produce plants with uniform colour and height? The answer is that we cannot grow a delphinium, from seed, that is completely identical to its parent or parents. Delphiniums are hybrids and do not breed true. Therefore, the only way in which such a plant can be obtained is by means of some form of vegetative propagation, from divisions, cuttings or eye cuttings. This allows us to increase our stock of favourite named cultivars or selected seedlings, without excessive difficulty and for moderate cost.

If you want to acquire a specific named cultivar you can only obtain it from an individual who propagates them vegetatively, or a delphinium specialist nursery. The cost of such a plant is higher than would be paid for a seedling in a garden centre, but its quality will be completely out of proportion and far better than the seedling alternative.

Vegetative propagation of delphiniums can be classified in three different ways. The first category is micro-propagation, which is a laboratory technique and cannot, therefore, be used by amateur growers. The chemicals used can produce mutated plants, not all of which will be desirable, of course, but it is notable that many hostas with unusual leaf patterns have been selected and introduced as a result of this process.

The second category is cuttings and eye cuttings. Taking and rooting these are fairly simple processes that are used by amateur gardeners and professional nurserymen alike. The advantage of these methods is that no part of the crown or roots of the parent plants, which are likely to contain some disease, are used. Completely new crowns and root systems are generated from the bases of the cuttings or eye cuttings.

The third category, division of an existing plant, is the easiest method of propagation. It is also the least satisfactory since various fungal and bacterial diseases will be included in the crown and root system, and will be propagated with it.

Whether you propagate your plants by division, taking cuttings or eye cuttings a sharp knife will be necessary. Cleanliness is next to godliness so that it is important that any risk of transmitting virus, fungal or bacterial diseases is minimised. For that reason a jar containing a hypochlorate solution such as 'Milton', obtainable from chemists, should be used to sterilise your knife between cuts.

Division

The standard method of propagating many herbaceous plants is by lifting and dividing them using a pair of forks placed back to back and then levered apart. In some cases, the root systems can simply be pulled apart. Matters are not so simple in the case of delphiniums because the roots, eyes and shoots grow from a hard solid crown, which lies just below soil level, which by its nature cannot normally be pulled apart but must be cut into healthy sections.

If you want to divide a delphinium, the best time to do it is in the spring between March and April. It is first necessary to lift the plant from the ground and then wash the soil from it, so that you can see what you are doing and assess its condition. The crown may be found reasonably healthy or may contain extensive rot in its centre. It will be seen that, on a mature large plant, the shoots and eyes are disposed around the outside edge. Examination of the lifted plant should suggest the places that it can be divided by downward cuts from a sharp knife.

After you have taken divisions from your plants, they should always be treated with a fungicide and potted up. This will allow you to check for any problems, or signs of poor health, as they grow and before they are planted out into the garden.

The problem with dividing delphinium plants is that you will also propagate bacterial and fungal infections, some types of virus, plain old fashioned rot as well as the plants. Therefore, this method of propagation really is not recommended. However, if you must use it, only divide healthy plants. You should examine any divisions carefully and discard any that contain rot.

You will obtain greatly superior results by taking conventional cuttings or eye cuttings, the methods of doing so being described in the sections that follow. The advantages being that no parts of the old crown or roots are used. New ones will be generated.

Taking cuttings

Mature delphinium plants should produce a considerable number of shoots in the spring. It is always advisable to thin those out, to produce fewer flowering spikes but of better quality and size. The best time to do this is when the shoots are 75 to 125 mm (3" to 5") long and 6 to 12 mm (0.25" to 0.5") in diameter, during February or March. The shoots that you remove can be used as cuttings, which can be rooted.

The first step is to decide which plants you want to propagate and then to scrape the soil away to expose the tops and sides of the crowns. To take the cuttings, it is essential that you use a strong and very sharp knife to cut the young shoots off, no higher than the point where they join the crown. If the cut is made too high up the stems, it will be found that the cuttings are hollow, or soft and pithy. If they are to root, they must have solid bases, with no holes, discernible softness or evidence of rot. Some growers include a heel or a very thin sliver of the crown, at the bottom of their cuttings, but this is not really necessary. A fine bladed scalpel can be used for trimming and tidying the cuttings, by removing decaying leaf scale at their bases as well as trimming off any large leaves that may have developed.

After the cuttings have been taken, the surrounding soil should be raked back around the delphinium plants, which should then be watered with fungicide that has been diluted in accordance with the manufacturer's recommendations.

The bases of the cuttings should be washed immediately and then inspected for dark discolouration, which would indicate the presence of rot or hollow cavities. If any is found, the cuttings should be discarded. If they appear satisfactory, their ends can be treated with a hormone powder such as 'synergol' before being inserted into a rooting medium. Whatever method you use, to root your cuttings, it is important to make sure that they are correctly labelled throughout the process.

If a small number of extra plants are wanted, this method of 'scrabbling' for cuttings amongst plants growing in the garden, is perfectly adequate even though getting down on your hands and knees is not ideal. Especially in wet weather or if you suffer from rheumatism or similar problems. An alternative is to dig up or lift plants, which can then be taken in to a greenhouse or potting shed where cuttings can be taken conveniently and in greater comfort. The lifted crowns may be plunged into peat or compost, in order that further cuttings can be removed periodically and as they develop. When the process of taking them has been finished, the exhausted crown must be disposed of.

Stock Plants

Professional nurseries propagate their delphiniums from stock plants that are grown specifically for that purpose. They are fertilised using potash and superphosphate to promote root growth and harder crowns. They should also be grown in fresh ground to minimise risks associated with soil borne bacteria, pests such as root lesion eelworms, and fungus diseases. The plants will be grown on from cuttings taken in the first year. They will then be lifted and removed to a propagating shed, in the winter and spring of the next, so that new cuttings or eye cuttings can be taken conveniently.

There is nothing to stop amateur growers from following similar procedures. Indeed, healthier plants can be obtained by doing so. The main problem is to find space for stock plants in an average garden. In larger ones, the kitchen garden areas can be used, growing your plants in rows that can be rotated annually with vegetables or other flowers. Another alternative is to grow your stock plants in large (we suggest 7.5 litre) pots, which contain mixtures of sterilised composts and loam to provide a healthy and disease free growing medium.

The traditional way to root cuttings

The traditional method of rooting cuttings is reliable, but fairly complicated, so that very few growers now follow this procedure, which involves use of a cold frame, with pure sharp sand incorporated into the top 75 mm (3") of soil. Sharp sand is then laid on top of that and the cuttings inserted into it. Alternatively, the cuttings can be inserted into pots containing mixtures of sharp sand, vermiculite and compost; plunging them into soil in the bottom of the cold frame. The cuttings should be kept moist but not excessively wet. The frame should be kept closed, except for turning the glass on top to reduce condensation. The cuttings will appear to flag just before rooting takes place within 4-6 weeks, but will perk up afterwards and start to grow. You should then provide progressively more ventilation, to harden the young plants off. Resist the temptation, at all times, to pull the cuttings out to see how they are doing, but once you are sure that rooting has taken place, from their growth, you should pot them up using a suitable compost.

There is a less elaborate, modern, alternative to using a cold frame for rooting cuttings in the traditional manner. That is to use a propagator without its cover and set on low heat. A compost made up of grit, sand and peat can be used that should be open in texture allowing a supply of ample air, as well as water, to the roots. The propagator can be sited in a greenhouse; which may however need shading as spring advances.

Water cuttings

The traditional method of rooting cuttings is labour intensive. A more convenient modern alternative is the water cutting method, which has a number of variations. It is especially suited to use by amateur gardeners but is also used professionally.

The simplest method is to take cuttings in the usual way and then place them in a small glass jar (the ones for fish paste or baby food are good) with a small quantity of sand or gravel and approximately 25 mm (1") of water. Place it in a position, inside the house, where it will receive plenty of light but is not exposed to direct sunlight. A jar can contain several cuttings, but be sure that they are all from the same cultivar and are clearly labelled, so that you know what they are. You can, of course, use this method in a shaded greenhouse, but will need to ensure that temperatures do not get too excessive.

The 'Perlite' method

A refinement of the water cutting method is to use small flowerpots filled with 'perlite', an expanded volcanic rock, into which the cuttings are inserted. These are stood on saucers or trays full of water that is drawn upwards by capillary action. Because the cuttings are contained in a moist and well-aerated medium, rooting should take place quickly. The cuttings should be watered initially from the top to establish a capillary action, using diluted fungicide.

If you need to root a large number of cuttings in a small space you can use 37 mm (1.5") moulded modules of the type used to grow plug plants. Those are filled with 'perlite' and then placed within gravel trays, which hold water. The water level can be monitored, by leaving one empty compartment at the corner of the tray.

Eye cuttings

Small buds, called eyes, are formed on the top and sides of a delphinium crown which, in the spring, will develop into shoots and then flowering stems. Their advocates suggest that because eye cuttings are usually very clean, free from rot and disease, they will develop better root systems.

Taking eye cuttings, before they develop into shoots, is reasonably straightforward. They are trimmed from the crown, being cut off (as with conventional cuttings) at the point where they join on to it. They are inserted (to about half their depth) into sterilised pots or trays that contain sharp sand, vermiculite or some similar rooting medium. They can be watered from above, or stood on saucers or trays containing water. It doesn't matter which so long as the eye cuttings and rooting medium are kept moist. We suggest that the water should contain diluted fungicide. After 4 to 6 weeks the tips of the eyes will become green and then start to grow, indicating that rooting has taken place.

Eye cuttings can be propagated at virtually any time during the growing season. The best time, traditionally, has been to take them in the summer, after the plant has flowered. However, some experts advocate lifting stock plants in January, rooting eye cuttings in greenhouses that have some heating. By doing this, decent sized young plants are produced that can be planted out in the late spring or early summer.

Potting up

However you propagate your delphiniums, whether from cuttings, eye cuttings or division, it is important that they should be potted up once they have rooted, so as to ensure that they are growing well. They should only be planted out into the garden once the young plants are growing strongly, in their pots, indicating successful rooting.

Cuttings, no matter what method you follow, whether traditional, water or perlite will take between 4 to 6 weeks for rooting to take place. The speed that they root will be dependent more on light levels than temperature, which should not exceed 15°C (60°F).

Whilst it is easy to see if a cutting has rooted in a glass jar, matters are not so easy if you are using the traditional 'cold frame' or modern 'perlite' methods. You should certainly resist the temptation to pull the cuttings out to take a look. Usually they won't look too healthy for a while, with the leaves looking sickly and dying back. But don't despair. The tips of the shoots will eventually start to green up and begin to grow. This is an indication that rooting has taken place. Wait a week to be sure, after which the cuttings can be transferred to clean and sterilised pots, using suitable sterilised compost. Afterwards, the primary shoot will start to grow and should then be disbudded, which is to say that the growing tip should be pinched out to allow the plants energies to be redirected into root development. This initial disbudding is absolutely vital for newly potted cuttings. It should always be done, irrespective of how the plant is grown on subsequently.

CHAPTER NINE

GROWING FROM SEED

By Patrick Booth

Growing elatum hybrid delphiniums from seed is undoubtedly the cheapest way to obtain a substantial stock of the plants. It is not difficult to do and the results can be interesting and rewarding.

There are two main pitfalls that you should be aware of. The first is that there is considerable variation in the quality, colour and form of delphiniums grown from seed. Therefore, your results will depend very much on the quality and pedigree of the seeds sown. If those are inherently inferior then no amount of careful cultivation will turn your plants into good ones. The best seeds will cost more, but not excessively so. The second requirement is that seeds must be stored correctly. If that is not done they will lose their viability and will not germinate or grow.

In the case of species delphiniums, growing from seeds can be more problematic since some will undoubtedly require special treatment. Species are interesting to grow but can be a challenge.

Choosing and obtaining seeds

Delphinium species usually have single florets and are normally cross-pollinated by bees and other insects. There is, however, a back-up mechanism so that, if they are not cross-pollinated, the flowers will be self-fertilised by their own pollen

Hybrid elatum delphiniums are artificial creations, their purpose being to look good and grow well. However, the structure of their florets prevents rather than helps most bees and other insects from transferring pollen between them. Modern cultivars have, however, retained the ability to self-pollinate.

If hybridisation or cross-fertilisation between different plants is required, florets must be pollinated by hand which is a laborious but rewarding process that allows hybridisers to select and combine desirable characteristics from two parent plants. In terms of seed strains, this is most likely to mean crossing similar ones in order to build up dominant characteristics, not only in terms of colour but also in such vital matters as hardiness and disease resistance. Generally speaking, delphiniums raised from hand-crossed seeds will benefit from hybrid vigour and also surpass the quality obtainable from self-pollinated seeds.

Commercially available seeds usually are self-pollinated. If they have been saved from good quality named cultivars, the seedlings obtained should be quite acceptable. Indeed, the normal seed sold by the Delphinium Society, and by specialist delphinium nurseries will have been saved from a carefully selected range of parent plants that are known to produce good offspring. There is nothing intrinsically wrong about saving and sowing self-pollinated seed from good quality plants.

There is no good reason therefore that so many commercially available seed strains are so generally poor. You should, in particular, be very wary of so-called 'Giant Pacific' seed strains or plants, which may flower true to colour but are likely to be of poor quality and not very perennial. Purchasing such seeds or the plants grown from them, which are often available in garden centres, is likely to result in disappointment even if you grow them well!

Hand-crossed seeds are another matter since whether they are obtained from a seed merchant or specialist source, there is at least some assurance that time and trouble has been taken to produce them. Hand-crossed seeds undoubtedly are the best obtainable. Although they cost more, the amount is not great if the number of plants that can be grown from them is taken into account. Such seeds are available commercially but can also be bought by its members from The Delphinium Society, which provides an autumn list of hand-crossed seeds to choose from.

Storing delphinium seeds

Successful germination of your delphinium seeds will depend very much on the way in which they have been stored. The assumption is often made that the elatum hybrid delphiniums must be tender because they are large and imposing plants, whereas genetically they are alpines from mountainous regions. Their seeds are adapted to withstand cold temperatures during the winter, but will not tolerate excessive warmth. Therefore, it is vital that they should always be placed in a sealed container (which should be clearly labelled since the seeds are poisonous) then stored in the main compartment of a refrigerator, not the freezer, until it is time to sow them.

Unfortunately, the problem with obtaining delphinium seeds from a garden centre, or shop, is that they usually have been placed in display racks, frequently in a warm and sunny spot, so that their ability to germinate will have been lost by the time of their purchase.

It is strongly recommended that you should purchase delphinium seeds direct from seed merchants rather than a rack in a garden centre. You will, however, usually get better seeds from a specialist delphinium nursery since their quality will be assured, whilst you can be certain that they have also been correctly stored.

Sowing and germinating seeds

Delphinium seeds are easy to germinate provided that they have been stored correctly and that the right temperature, not too cold and definitely not too warm is maintained after they have been sown.

Seeds can be sown at any time during the growing season. The traditional time to do it was in late summer and early autumn, using freshly harvested seed. This is an old practice from a time, pre-dating use of refrigerators, when it was difficult to store seed properly and retain its viability until the spring. Seeds can, obviously still be sown in the late summer and this will allow a good flowering to be obtained the following June or July. However, there are considerable difficulties in over wintering small plants and protecting them from slugs.

Our recommendation, nowadays, is for seeds, previously stored in a refrigerator, to be sown in March. There would be sufficient but not excessive warmth for them to germinate quickly and for the resulting seedlings to be grown on for the rest of the season. Indeed, given decent cultivation, fully representative flower spikes can be obtained within six months from sowing. In Britain, winters have become increasingly mild which tempts us to sow seed earlier. If you wish to do this we suggest that half the seeds should be sown, the remainder to be stored in the refrigerator for sowing at the usual time.

Seeds can be sown in pots, seed trays or propagators. If those have been used previously then it is important that they should be cleaned and washed with a good general sterilant, such as 'Milton', which is available from chemists or 'Jeyes Fluid' which is available from garden centres, to prevent the spread of disease and infection.

The compost used should be a sterilised type, so that there are no possible soil borne infections and no chance of the young seedlings being confused with emerging weed seeds. It does not matter what type of seed compost you use, just stick to your favourite. Delphinium seeds will germinate equally well in peat based such as 'Levington' or 'Arthur Bowers', or freshly obtained soil based 'John Innes' types. Some growers prefer to mix 'vermiculite' or 'perlite' into the compost since this makes it more water retentive, whilst maintaining good aeration. It is important that seeds should not be sown too deeply; but rather just covered with a thin layer of compost or vermiculite.

When you have sown your seeds, firm the surface of the compost gently. They should then be watered regularly to ensure that they do not dry out. Fungicide should be added to the water, to prevent seedlings from 'damping off'.

The tray or pot containing the seeds should be put somewhere cool for germination to take place. It is vital that the seeds should not get too hot, since this is the most common cause of failure. You should aim to keep the temperature within the range of 3°C to a maximum of 15°C (40°F to 60°F). Delphinium seeds should germinate within 2 to 3 weeks. The first thing that you will see will be a pair of seed leaves, otherwise known as cotyledons. Those are rounded in shape and look nothing like the true leaves which will start to appear about a week later.

Finally, it is absolutely essential to protect your young seedlings against slugs, since an entire tray full represents no more than a light snack and can disappear in very short order.

Sowing under glass

If delphinium seeds are sown in March and given good cultivation, then decent flower spikes can be seen 6 months later, from September onwards.

Good quality maiden spikes can be obtained earlier, if seeds are sown in January or early February, within a greenhouse. The advantages of doing so are that flowers will be obtained in July or August, when the main delphinium spikes are not usually available. More importantly, larger plants will be built up for flowering the following year.

The disadvantages of sowing under glass are that the process is more labour intensive with a particular need to maintain, but not exceed, the ideal temperatures for germination by providing some form of background heat.

Chitting seeds

Germinating elatum hybrid delphinium seeds in the conventional way is a simple and reliable process. Some other seeds, however, including many delphinium species can be more difficult.

Chitting seed is an alternative to sowing in compost. The process consists of pre-germinating seeds on a wet paper towel, placed in a container, which can then be kept in a room or cupboard where temperatures can be maintained correctly.

The seeds should be examined daily. Any that have germinated can then be transferred carefully, using tweezers, into small pots containing compost. This has the advantage that 'pricking out' is avoided later.

Although elatum hybrid delphiniums are easy to grow from seed by conventional methods, some prefer to 'chit' them anyway arguing that better control of the temperature, at which they are germinated, is possible. Close observation of the germinating seeds can be made so that they can be easily transferred to small pots at the appropriate time, eliminating the pricking out stage in which some root damage can occur to your small plants.

Pricking out and potting up

Young seedling plants should be pricked out when they appear sturdy enough. Usually, this will be when 2 true leaves have developed. Pricking out should not be delayed, since the roots of young seedlings grow very quickly to become intertwined, making separation of the young plants difficult.

Always ensure that clean pots are used. Be prepared to clean them, as with seed trays, with a good garden sterilant. 7.5 cm (3") pots are best initially, filled with sterilised potting compost of whatever type you personally favour.

Plastic pots will be adequate but plants can get very hot in them. Terracotta pots are porous, will keep plants cooler and will breathe better, but are more expensive. 'Crocking' the bases of the pots is important, to give good drainage. Broken terracotta pots can be used, or alternatively rough stones of suitable size, always taking care that they do not block the hole at the bottom of the pot.

You should resist the temptation to use liquid fertilisers on tiny seedlings. However, once they have been potted on and become reasonably sturdy, then we recommend that a dilute high potash/phosphate fertiliser can be used in accordance with manufacturer's recommendations. It is also important to keep very small seedlings shaded, so that direct sunlight doesn't cause them to collapse. As the plants grow more sizeable, however, they can be placed in full sun but should be watered regularly.

BREEDING PRINCIPLES AND OPPORTUNITIES

By David Bassett

Delphiniums for our gardens may come from friends, garden shops or specialist nurserymen but it can be particularly exciting to raise the plants oneself from seed. There is often a degree of uncertainty about what colour the flowers of seedlings will be and how tall the blooms will grow. This fascinating variability of seedlings also provides every delphinium enthusiast with the opportunity to directly influence the characteristics of the flowers and to work towards plants with flowers of a favourite colour and form.

The basic procedure for such delphinium breeding is to collect seeds from a plant that most nearly resembles your favourite flower and then raise a new batch of seedlings. When these flower, select the best and use seeds saved from it for the next generation of plants. Delphinium seedlings can be flowered and evaluated within a few months of sowing the seed, so the time between the generations can be as short as two years. This is a distinct advantage for amateur gardeners because you see results and make progress much sooner than with roses or paeonies.

There are two crucial elements in this breeding procedure: 'sex' and 'selection'. In sexual reproduction of delphiniums, the genetic characters of a seed parent (female) are combined with the genetic characters of a pollen parent (male) when an ovule is fertilised by a pollen grain and subsequently develops to a seed. An important aspect of breeding is that we can choose the parents and make deliberate crosses by hand-pollination of flowers. The range of characteristics seen in seedlings raised from such crosses depends on how genetic characters of both parents are combined in the seeds. Before considering the details, it is necessary to look first at 'selection' because this contribution made by the plant breeder ultimately determines the success or failure of a breeding programme.

Objectives and selection

The first step is to decide on an objective for your delphinium breeding. Keep this simple so that it corresponds to a well-defined genetic character that can be easily recognised when assessing seedlings. Avoid setting objectives that relate to complex, multi-faceted aspects of delphinium character, however worthwhile they may appear. The longevity of delphiniums, for example, depends on both physiological characteristics of the plants and environmental factors that cannot be adequately controlled in a garden situation.

A good example of a well-defined objective is to seek a particular colour for either the sepals or the eye-petals of the flower. You could equally well focus on aspects of flower form, perhaps by requiring that blooms have a broadly pyramidal shape or looking for a large number of secondary flower stems. Another reasonable aim would be to develop plants that flower either exceptionally early or late relative to the normal flowering time for garden delphiniums, although this character would not be immediately apparent when seedlings flower for the first time.

When the objective is clear, it is possible to examine a batch of seedlings and to identify those plants with the desired character. For example, if the objective is white flowers with light brown eyes, then a cross between two cultivars with light brown eyes, 'Olive Poppleton', a white flower and 'Emily Hawkins', a related plant with violet flowers, should yield a small proportion of seedlings of the appropriate colour. There is also a chance of white flowers with light brown eyes if you raise plants from seeds collected from either of these cultivars, even when the flowers are not hand-pollinated. The real skill of a delphinium breeder comes in selecting one or two plants from the group of seedlings having white flowers with light brown eyes that will be the best to use in further breeding. Although their flowers are similar in colour, the plants may differ in floret form, spike shape and regularity, height and vigour of the growth or susceptibility to mildew. All such factors should be considered when making selections and this requires a detailed knowledge of the parent plants as well as the general features of a good delphinium.

Sex and inheritance

It is possible to breed delphiniums without understanding the mechanism by which specific characters are passed from one generation to the next but it is useful to know a little about what is involved. The idea that the genetic character of plants and animals is coded in DNA, with each genetically distinct individual having a unique DNA fingerprint, is now very familiar.

Chromosomes contain DNA and the nucleus of each plant cell generally contains two copies of each chromosome, one from each parent. Such a plant is said to be diploid. Delphinium species are usually diploid but cultivated forms with larger numbers of chromosomes appeared at some stage in the development of modern garden delphiniums. The so-called elatum hybrid cultivars are tetraploid, and there are 32 chromosomes in the nucleus of each plant cell. These represent 4 copies of the basic set of 8 distinct types of chromosome that can be seen in the nuclei when cells are examined with a microscope. Belladonna delphiniums may be infertile triploids, with 3 sets of chromosomes or fertile hexaploids with 6 sets.

Chromosomes can be thought of as a string of beads. Each bead corresponds to a gene, which directs the chemical synthesis of a molecule with a specific molecular structure, such as an enzyme. This enzyme then determines a particular character of the plant by facilitating and controlling steps in chemical relations occurring in plant cells during some aspect of growth and development, like germination of the seed, flower bud development or seed production.

It is desirable to select well-defined objectives for delphinium breeding because there is then a chance that we focus attention on a character of the plant that is determined either by a single gene or possibly a number of genes acting together. For example, evidence from breeding delphiniums like 'Sunkissed' suggests that creamy yellow flowers are abnormal and associated with a fundamental change in pigmentation controlled by a single gene. Very dramatic demonstrations of flower characteristics controlled by a single gene can be seen when a chance mutation causes a small change in the gene and results in a different colour for the flower or 'colour sport'. Sometimes the changes are limited in scope, as for sports of 'Emily Hawkins' with flowers having a black eye instead of the normal light brown one. In other cases a change in eye colour may be accompanied by changes in flower colour, as seen in a mutation that changed the sepal colour of a blue flower to pale pink and the eye from black to white. Florets can sometimes be found with both the normal colouring and the 'sport' in separate sectors.

A crucial feature of sexual reproduction is that an ovule or pollen grain contains only half the number of chromosomes of a normal cell, i.e. one set of 8 chromosomes for a species delphinium but two sets (16 chromosomes) for a cultivated elatum hybrid. An important point for a tetraploid delphinium is that the 2 sets of chromosomes are selected randomly from the 4 sets in an ordinary plant cell. The two sets of chromosomes from a pollen grain are added to the ovule during fertilisation, which restores the number of chromosome sets to 4. The seed that develops and the plants grown from it therefore have a random selection of the genes from seed and pollen parents.

It might be thought that the presence of genes from both parents in every plant cell would lead to plants with characters intermediate between those of the parents. Studies of plant genetics made long before the existence of genes was known about established that this is not the normal situation and introduced the concept that an observable character of a plant could be either dominant or recessive. For example, in the typical flower of a wild delphinium there are 5 sepals and the flower is said to be 'single' but many elatum cultivars have 'semi-double' flowers with 13 sepals. The number of sepals is a character that is easily checked and, for tetraploid elatum hybrids, when a 'semi-double' is crossed with a 'single', at least 50% of the resulting seedlings are found to be 'single'. In this case 'single' is the dominant form of the character and is seen, while 'semi-double' is recessive and is unseen, although all the 'singles' among the seedlings contain both forms of the gene that controls the number of sepals.

Unfortunately, most of the characters of delphiniums that we consider desirable for a garden plant tend to be recessive, while bad features are usually dominant. The chances of raising plants with all the good qualities we seek are therefore low and there is a substantial risk that desirable features will be lost when plants are raised from seed produced by random pollination of flowers.

Continuing with the example of sepal number and assuming that the character is associated with a single gene, then this gene must have two forms, which can be labelled 'S' for the dominant or 's' for the recessive form. Since a recessive character can only be seen if the dominant form of the gene involved is not present, all the four chromosomes in a cell nucleus of a tetraploid 'semi-double' delphinium must contain the recessive form of the gene, so the set of genes for sepal number is 'ssss'. For a plant with 'single' flowers, however, the gene set could be 'Ssss', 'SSss', 'SSSs' or 'SSSS' since the presence of even a single copy of the dominant gene determines the character of the plant.

To see the significance of the composition of the gene sets in the parents of a cross, it is useful to look further at the inheritance of sepal number. Consider first a cross with one parent being a 'semi-double' flower, which is the recessive form for sepal number so that the set of genes must be 'ssss'. A random selection of two chromosomes from the set of four can be made in six ways, so ovules or pollen grains from this cultivar will have the gene set 'ss'. For the other parent we could use an exceptionally pretty 'single' flower derived from a previous cross between a 'semi-double' and a 'single'. Let us suppose that the 4 chromosomes have the gene set 'SSss'. Selecting two of the chromosomes randomly, ovules or pollen grains can have a variety of different gene sets, 'SS', 'Ss'(x4) (i.e. 4 sets of this type), 'ss'. If we use this 'single' flower as the seed parent and fertilise the ovules with pollen from the 'semi-double', then seeds can have chromosome sets with sepal number gene sets, 'SSss', 'Ssss'(x4), 'ssss'. Only seeds with the last of these sets will give rise to semi-double flowers, as they have no copy of the dominant gene in any of the four chromosomes. These represent one sixth of the seeds, i.e. 16.7% of the seedlings that can be raised. It should be noted that the result would be the same if the 'semi-double' were used as the seed parent.

To a beginner, this low percentage of 'semi-double' seedlings might seem somewhat discouraging. It is, however, a quite favourable case. If you chose to cross the 'single' to itself, the sepal number gene sets for both ovules and pollen would be 'SS', 'Ss'(x4), and 'ss'. There is now only one combination of the pairs out of the 36 possible combinations that generates the set 'ssss' which would result in a plant with 'semi-double' flowers. To have only about 3% of the seedlings with 'semi-double' flowers from such a cross between parents that both have a double dose of the recessive gene for such a desirable flower character demonstrates well the potential for frustration inherent in breeding delphiniums when tetraploid genetics apply. There are two possible conclusions to be drawn from this: one is that to obtain a worthwhile number of seedlings exhibiting the recessive form of a genetic trait hidden in cross parents that exhibit the dominant form, it will generally be necessary to grow hundreds of plants of the cross. The other conclusion is that there is a huge advantage to be gained from making crosses where one parent is of the recessive type and the other has at least two and preferably three doses of the recessive gene involved. In the latter case, yields of seedlings with the desired character can be up to 50% and it is then possible to make selections between them for other desirable features when growing only 25-50 seedlings of a particular cross.

Of course no delphinium comes with a label saying it has a triple dose of the recessive gene for some particular trait, so how is any breeder to obtain such information? The answer lies in keeping quite detailed records about the characteristics of all seedlings grown from known seed parents. An apparently unusual seedling, such as a pink flower among seedlings from the pale violet cultivar 'Emily Hawkins' or a creamy-yellow flower among seedlings from the deep dusky pink 'Lucia Sahin' is significant. It shows that these cultivars contain in their chromosomes some doses of the recessive genes for pink flowers and creamy-yellow flowers respectively. Such chance observations should not be ignored as they can often lead a breeding programme in exciting new directions as you attempt to follow them up.

For hand-pollinated crosses, the percentages of seedlings with a particular recessive character are a direct indicator of both the presence of a recessive gene and the number of doses of this in the gene sets for the cross parents. Approximately half the seedlings from a cross between 'Royal Flush' and any creamy yellow delphinium, e.g. 'Sungleam', have creamy-yellow flowers, which indicates that 'Royal Flush' hides a triple dose of the recessive gene for the pigmentation change that provides creamy-yellow flowers.

The scope for delphinium breeding in a small garden

If delphiniums become fashionable flowers in the future, advanced genetic engineering procedures will probably allow professional breeders plants with novel types of growth habit and flowers in colours not attainable by traditional breeding methods. Amateur growers may dream of making such breakthroughs, but the most that we can realistically expect to achieve are small improvements in the qualities of the plants already available.

The obvious target for improvement by making hand-pollinated crosses between selected plants remains the elatum hybrid cultivars. There is little point in generating plants looking exactly like existing named cultivars available to you but it is worthwhile to seek replacements for old cultivars and cultivars never available where you live. Outside Britain, even the most famous 'English Delphiniums', such as 'Blue Nile', are hardly ever available and it is then sensible to start from seed and raise comparable cultivars that would be better suited to the local climatic conditions.

Giant 2.5 mtrs (8'0") tall delphiniums can be a spectacular attraction so long as the wind does not blow but, in breeding, we should seek plants with a more practical growth habit. First, we should ask ourselves if an enormously long flower spike is really necessary. Secondly, we need to select plants with slim, tough stems and a short distance between leaf joints, so that the blooms rise above a compact mound of foliage. Plants with short-jointed stems can be raised but it is essential to check the effect of environment on them. Just when you think you might have produced good seedlings with this character, heavy rain during bloom development or competition with tall adjacent plants can force the stems up to unexpected heights!

Stem branching is another aspect of growth habit deserving attention. Flowers developing on side-shoots (or laterals) of the white cultivar 'Lilian Bassett', for example, prolong the display for an exceptionally long period. It is encouraging that a large number of side-shoots seems to be a dominant character in crosses made using 'Lilian Bassett'. However, side shoots are of little value unless they are sufficiently sturdy to withstand bad weather.

The form and colour of florets are favourite subjects for all breeders. You can choose parents for crosses to attain any desired result, whether it is sepals with smoothly rounded or frilly edges, an exceptionally large number of petals in the eye, or even 'double' flowers in which the distinction between sepals and eye petals is lost. One can also make crosses between cultivars of similar colour, looking for improvements in the clarity or brightness of the colouring. Do not, however, expect to make breakthroughs to colours like clear pinks and true reds just by crossing existing dusky pink elatum cultivars. That approach is unlikely to produce the change probably necessary in the pigmentation chemistry of the flowers. There is a great deal of fun to be had from making crosses between flowers of distinctly different colour. Crossing violet flowers with dusky pinks, for example, can lead you to colour patterning seldom seen in named cultivars, such as strong veining or picotee edging to the sepals.

Turning to other types of cultivated delphinium, there is scope for breeding new Belladonna-type cultivars. One could look for improvements in the range of colours and the growth habit of plants by making crosses between fertile cultivars, just as for elatum hybrids. Plants are already available with white flowers or flowers in shades of blue, including wonderfully brilliant gentian blues, so why not try to extend the range to pinks and purples. Flowers can also be found with unusual types of eye, so there are many variations to work with.

Another interesting group of cultivated delphiniums is the range of dwarf strains generally described as *Delphinium grandiflorum var chinense*. Such plants are now of considerable interest to the nursery trade because of their suitability for pot culture and late summer sales. It should be possible to make crosses that lead to new colours, larger florets and better growth habit for these delightful miniatures. A good way to start is to raise a collection of plants from commercially available seed strains, which already provide good blues, white, purple and pinkish shades. When the plants flower, select those with interesting colour or especially good form and, remembering that these delphiniums are best treated as annuals, immediately make a few crosses between them.

A final thought about breeding delphiniums: when you fail to get a tingle of excitement from the brilliance of a blue, or the clarity of an icing-sugar pink seen as the first florets of a new seedling open, just stop.

A 'Rosemary Brock x Lucia Sahin' seedling: Raised from Delphinium Society seed. A list of hand-crossed and other seeds is sent to members, each autumn, for them to choose from. The seedling shown demonstrates the quality that can be obtained from such seeds.

A diagram showing the components of a single flowered delphinium.

A diagram showing the various parts of a semi-double delphinium.

Hybridisation: The six photographs show different stages in hand-crossing seeds:

1. Removing a few sepals from a floret reveals eye-petals and anthers.
2. The immature pollen anthers and the eye-petals are removed by a quick nip with your fingernails.
3. When the stigmas have widened and show a sticky appearance (visible with a magnifying glass) they are ready for pollination..
4. A floret from a potential pollen parent, with anthers shedding pollen. This can be pressed against the stigmas of the seed parent's florets to effect pollination.
5. Alternatively, pollen can be transferred to receptive stigmas using an artist's brush. Pollen can be seen adhering to the stigmas as the brush is withdrawn.
6. After a few days, fertilisation results in swelling of the seed-pods. Three to four weeks after fertilisation the pods will change colour to yellowish or brown tints as the seed ripens.

An 'Olive Poppleton x Lilian Bassett' seedling: Once again, demonstrating the quality of plants that can be obtained from hand-crossed seeds, in this case, obtained from The Delphinium Society.

A 'Loch Nevis x H.G. Mills' seedling: An attractive plant with double, gentian blue florets, raised by Duncan McGlashan. The plant was, however, discarded. Looking good is obviously an important requirement for a named cultivar. However it must also grow well, perform reliably and be perennial.

'Fenella' There are no concerns about 'Fenella', which is quite an old cultivar, raised by Blackmore and Langdon and introduced in 1964. It received an Award of Merit in 1968. It continues to perform well, with little sign of deterioration.

A 'Rosemary Brock x Lucia Sahin' seedling

A 'SINGLE' FLORET

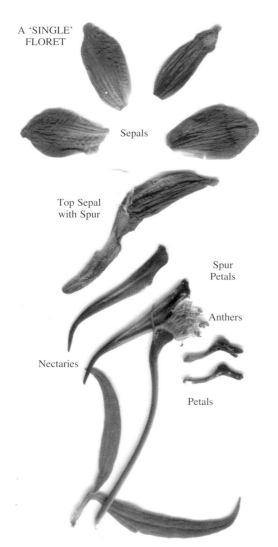

Sepals

Top Sepal with Spur

Spur Petals

Anthers

Nectaries

Petals

A diagram showing the components of a single flowered delphinium

ni-double
floret   'Gordon Forsyth'

SEPALS   8 Inner
                                          Sepals

5 Outer
Sepals

Spur

Anthers   Spur petal
                     with nectary

Petals

A diagram showing the various parts of a semi-double delphinium

1. Eye-petals and anthers ready for removal

2. Emasculation reveals immature carpels

3. Receptive stigmas ready for pollination

4. Floret with anthers shedding pollen

5. Pollen can be transferred to stigmas using artists' brush

6. Ripening seed pods

An 'Olive Poppleton x Lilian Bassett' seedling

A 'Loch Nevis x H.G. Mills' seedling

'Fenella'

CHAPTER ELEVEN

HAND-CROSSING AND HYBRIDISING DELPHINIUMS

By Duncan McGlashan

Firstly, why should we bother with making hand-crosses when we know that the open pollinated seed from our named plants gives good results? It is widely accepted that hand-crossed seed gives better results in the main but, more importantly, this gives at least some control over colour, form and other desirable characteristics, even though, given the complex genetics of our modern delphiniums the results are something of a lottery. The choice of parents for hand crosses is, therefore, very much a matter of individual choice.

We are fortunate that elatum hybrid delphiniums are relatively easy to cross with other cultivars and some of the delphinium species. In particular the basic mechanics of hand-crossing are simple: so much so that it has been said a reasonably intelligent orang-utan could manage this procedure. Perhaps a little fanciful but it does make the point that any prospective hybridiser need not fear that any great demands will be made either in terms of manual dexterity or indeed brain power! What is needed are the simple virtues of attention to detail, concentration and patience. Before discussing hand crossing perhaps we should first consider how, left to their own devices, delphiniums set seed.

Outline of delphinium natural seed production

Delphinium florets comprise one or two rows of coloured outer sepals, formed from the outer casing of the flower bud. The eye, or bee, at the centre of each floret is formed from the true petals. Male (pollen bearing anthers) and female (stigma, style and ovaries) reproductive organs lie at the centre of each floret, behind the eye petals.

As the florets open, the male pollen anthers can be seen just inside and underneath the eye or inner petals, right in the centre of the floret. The female styles and ovaries lie beneath the pollen anthers. These are undeveloped at this stage and, indeed, are not even visible.

Fairly soon after the floret has opened, and depending on climatic conditions, the anthers may start to produce pollen but become spent and cease doing so after 2-3 days. At this stage the styles are nowhere near producing receptive stigma. In fact it could be a week or so before they become receptive thus allowing fertilisation.

It appears that, left to their own devices, our elatum delphiniums self-pollinate, which suggests that shed pollen can survive in the central cluster for several days. We have seen experimental evidence that ripe pollen can survive in-vitro for as long as two weeks. If we accept that our delphiniums do, usually, self fertilise it is obvious that pollen must be able to survive on the central cluster for maybe a week or so.

As we noted before we have evidence that pollen can be stored for two weeks and remain viable. It is, however, still remarkable that under outdoor conditions pollen can withstand wind and rain, yet still effect pollination.

Our own experiments have shown that pollen applied to the styles/stigma some four days before full stigma receptivity effected pollination. It is now widely accepted (though not by all!) that insects, including bees, play little or no part in the natural fertilisation of elatum hybrid delphiniums. The suggested mechanism is that the bisexual florets/flowers simply self-pollinate, certainly in the main. This topic has caused considerable controversy in the past, with some acrimonious debate in the Delphinium Society Year Book (if you enjoy a good botanical row try to obtain a copy of the 1962 edition). However, no less an authority than Bob Legro has stated that elatum hybrids mostly self-pollinate and that, although the humble-bee can pollinate elatums (unlike other bee species), this rarely happens in practice.

What is important for our hand crossing efforts is that the stigma have a much slower development than pollen production by the anthers. This makes hybridisation simple, i.e. all you have to do is remove the pollen anthers before any pollen is shed and then apply ripe pollen from the other parent as the stigma nears or reaches receptivity.

Producing hand-crossed seed has, perhaps in broad outline, 5 stages:
1. *Pre-planning* by choosing the parents to be used and ensuring that the chosen maternal and paternal parents will be available at the right time.
2. *Preparing the maternal parents* by removing the immature pollen anthers before pollen production.
3. *Applying the chosen paternal pollen* to the prepared florets of the maternal parent, with the stigma near or at receptive phase.
4. *Care and protection* of the developing seed pods.
5. *Harvesting the ripe seed*, cleaning and storage.

Stages in detail

Pre-planning

This is essential. Examine your plants before the basal florets or spikes/laterals open. Decide whether to use spikes or laterals. Our own preference is to use main spikes since this will give you a greater certainty of success and, of course, more seed. If you only require a small number of seeds, using laterals makes sense and avoids disfiguring the main spikes.

Do make sure that that you will have a good supply of the paternal pollen for some time after preparing the maternal florets. Remember, too, if a particular cross is a high priority it can be useful to cross both ways, i.e. prepare florets of both parents by emasculation and make sure that there are enough florets to produce pollen from both parents at the right time.

Preparation of maternal parents

As the florets are just opening, or shortly before natural opening, open up the florets. The immature pollen anthers and the eye petals are removed by a quick nip with your fingernails. With care this is quite safe since at this time the styles and ovaries are completely undeveloped and well down in the centre cluster. Some hybridists prefer to use forceps. Provided you remove the anthers and eye petals it does not matter how you do it.

Some prefer to remove all the floret petals leaving only the immature styles/ovaries in a central cluster on the pedicel i.e. the 'nude' floret, the rationale being that the stem with just pedicels and the small cluster of styles is not likely to attract insects. Our own occasional use of this method is based upon the fact that such stems stand up to even the strongest winds!

One important point is to make quite sure that the pollen anthers are still immature. One or two maverick cultivars, such as 'Gossamer' can start to produce pollen before the floret opens. Therefore, it is important to discard any such florets and to rinse your hands at intervals during this process.

Applying the paternal parent pollen to the emasculated maternal parent

The time it takes for the styles to enlarge, lengthen and develop receptive stigma varies to some degree with different plants, especially so with climatic conditions, but will usually be some days after the florets open. The florets should be checked every day to assess style/stigma development. At first it is a slow process but, when the styles start to lengthen at the tips, the stigma may become receptive quite quickly. Some hybridists inspect the prepared florets with a magnifier and only apply pollen when they observe the signs of fully receptive stigma. These are when the stigma have widened and show a sticky lobed appearance. We think that this carries some risk, certainly for the novice, since the fully receptive phase can be quite short.

Our approach is to start applying pollen maybe three days before the stigma become receptive and to continue with this every day until it is obvious that the cross has worked (or failed). You should get a good harvest with this approach. We have in fact successfully used a single application of pollen four days before the stigma became receptive, confirming that pollen can remain viable in the floret for several days.

As to the pollen scource, most hybridists simply gather fresh florets of the paternal parent, which are starting to show pollen. The eye petals are pulled back and the central cluster of anthers loaded with pollen is then gently dabbed on to the stigma. A well-laden cluster of ripe pollen anthers can be used for a good number of florets, as the actual amount of pollen required to effect fertilisation is very small. There is, with some rather less fertile plants, evidence that really heavy 'caking' with pollen can sometimes produce seed even with delphiniums of very low fertility.

Some hybridists prefer to use a brush, which is loaded with the relevant pollen and gently dabbed on the stigma. Obviously the brush must be cleaned with each change of pollen, but that is also true of the alternative, which is the simple manual method, when hands should be rinsed and dried between different crosses. We do not think that it matters how you apply the pollen provided it works for you and avoids cross contamination.

We do have some concern about the common practice of using florets that have started to produce pollen whilst on plants in the open. Apart from the obvious risk of losing pollen by wind or rain, it does increase the chance of cross contamination. As we have said insects and/or wind drift are not major factors but are possibly important, especially if you experience that wretched little insect, the pollen beetle. It is not so much a matter of the pollen that they consume but the fact that they move from plant to plant, thus creating a risk of cross contamination.

Our solution is simple and gives a greater certainty that the pollen is uncontaminated and is always available, both dry and viable. The paternal florets are picked when they are about to open or just before. They are then opened up and placed in small trays and stored in warm, dry conditions, for example a greenhouse or shed. We find it better to place the florets face down. The floret sepals dry up in a couple of days, but the pollen anthers with most cultivars start, usually, to produce copious amounts of pollen. Such pollen, if kept dry, usually remains viable for two weeks or more. Thus this simple method gives a greater degree of certainty and maximum yields.

Another method uses plants in pots, which can be moved into a cold greenhouse so that the risk of rain and wind damage is removed. It is easier, particularly in wet or windy weather, to work in a greenhouse, especially if you hope to produce hand crossed seed in quantity.

It is usually fairly obvious as to whether or not successful fertilisation has occurred. Firstly the styles/seed pods start to show rapid growth. The failures show no such growth and, indeed, often start to shrivel. Some plants also show failures by the crossing over of the styles. However, some cultivars do this before and after successful fertilisation. The key point is rapid growth.

Care and protection of the seed pods

It is now important to consider how to protect the precious developing seed pods. It is perhaps only when you take up delphinium hybridising that you become aware of how many diverse predators of pods and seed exist. This includes birds, specifically the bullfinch, and several insects including certain moth caterpillars together with earwigs and climbing snails. Bullfinches can cause severe damage to seedpods. They usually attack the pods whilst they are still green and with nearly mature seed. What is especially trying is that these finches only eat the seed at the apex of the pod before moving on to the next one. The result is ingress of moisture via the damaged seed pod, which renders the remaining immature seed useless. The only answer is to cover your stems with a coarse weave hood or net. Garden netting works quite well. It is important to use coarse weave so as to allow good air circulation and also so as not to provide cover for earwigs. Both earwigs and caterpillars can cause major losses of the developing seed, the only really effective answer being to use a good systemic insecticide. If you are not able or willing to use insecticides, then the only answer is frequent and vigilant inspections of plants and seed pods, hand picking the pests whenever you find them.

The time taken for the seed to become ripe enough to harvest varies considerably with climate. There are, also, some differences between cultivars, but it will be some time, anything between three and five weeks, from successful pollination.

Harvesting the ripe seed

With many cultivars the seed pods are ready to harvest when the pods become yellow/brown and start to open at the apex. Other cultivars can show seed pods, which are still green and yet contain ripe seed i.e. dark brown or black. In both cases the seed pods should be picked at once. Daily inspections should be made as the seed pods, when ripe, often open and can shed seed. Also, the open pod end will allow water in, which often leads to mildew, thus ruining the seed.

A simple test to check whether the seed pods are ready to harvest is the PST or pod seam test. This simply consists of applying gentle pressure to the seam, which runs the full length of the pod. If the seeds are ripe the pod will open showing dark brown or black seed, ready for harvesting. If the seed inside is still unripe it usually takes considerable pressure to open the pod. Each spike or lateral will, of course, produce ripe seed pods in succession so that the harvesting of a particular spike may well take place over a week or more. This means it is convenient initially to place the seed pods as they are harvested into an envelope or some other suitable container. The most important point here is to make sure that the envelopes or containers are clearly marked with the details of the cross.

After a few days, transfer the seed into a small dish – plastic petri dishes are very suitable. Keep in a warm, dry atmosphere. In a few days the pods dry out and it is quite easy to separate the seeds from the remains of the pod. If available, suitable sieves are very useful so that clean seeds with no dust or dross are obtained.

Before storage, examine the seeds carefully and remove any showing signs of mildew. Then place the precious seed in plastic re-sealable envelopes which are air and watertight. If you use ordinary paper envelopes do make sure that these are stored in an air-tight and waterproof container. The containers should be stored in a refrigerator at 4 degrees centigrade. All that remains is to wait until it is time to sow the seed.

Finally, as the Zen Buddhist says, "there are many paths to salvation"! There are also several methods of producing hand-crossed seed. All we can say is that the method described has enabled one individual to produce 350,000 hand-crossed seeds in one season. Of one thing we are certain, whether you decide to grow 50,000 seedlings or just 50, you will find seeing your own crosses in flower to be a very rewarding experience. Good luck!

ASSESSMENT OF SEEDLINGS

By Nigel Moody and Les Cooper

Irrespective of whether delphiniums are grown from self-pollinated or hand-crossed seeds they will show considerable variation in terms of colour, plant architecture and perenniality. Selecting which seedlings to retain depends very much on your desired aims. If you have grown them merely to "rogue" the worst examples from the batch and plant the rest around the herbaceous border, then the resulting selection is entirely personal and will conform to your own particular likes and dislikes.

If you are selecting possible cultivars for cut flower purposes, the prime requirements are likely to be that the plants should exhibit good flower holding properties. You may prefer the florets to be slightly proud (i.e. looking slightly upwards) rather than facing at right angles to the main flowering spike, since this will make packing them in cellophane over-wraps somewhat easier and less likely to cause floret damage.

For most people, selection is based on the hope that some seedlings will ultimately be good enough to be propagated, named and entered into commerce. Although personal taste will still have an influence on the selection, there are quite a number of criteria to consider. A few pointers are listed in the following sections, which will assist in determining the chosen few.

Constitution and perenniality

Good constitution and perenniality in a plant is essential. It matters not what other desirable properties the plant may have. If it is not vigorous and does not continue to grow well for a number of years, then it should be discarded since it will always require nursing.

The vigour of delphiniums does vary within colour groups. For example, cream delphiniums are always less vigorous than others. Accordingly if you believe a cream seedling of yours to be a potential winner, grow it next to an established and recognised 'good' cream and compare the vigour. If it is to be named, your seedling should possess a constitution and perenniality at least as good, and preferably better than, the established named cultivar.

The performance of delphiniums can vary depending on soil conditions. A plant, which grows superbly on a certain type of soil, may grow miserably elsewhere. A way of testing for this trait is to give plants to trusted delphinium friends in other parts of the country, and to compare results.

Plant architecture

The spike length of a delphinium should always be a pleasing proportion of the plant's height. There are a number of delphiniums in commerce where the blooms look superb when cut and placed on the show bench but are hideous in the garden, with the spike peering out at the top of an enormously long stem. We call them 'toothbrush delphiniums'. Ideally for garden purposes the spike length should be 50% or more of the total plant height but should not be less than 40%.

Shorter growing cultivars are to be preferred, in general, since they fit better into today's smaller gardens and are less liable to wind damage. There are some delphiniums (an example being 'Mighty Atom') that have a compact mound of foliage, occupying a mere 33% of the overall plant height, which some consider to be a good, classical proportion.

Ideally the delphinium spike should be broader at the base and taper off at the top, ending in a point. The degree to which this is acceptable really depends on the length of the spikes produced by the cultivar. Shorter spikes look rather ugly if their bases are much broader than their tops.

The placement of florets is important. They should be arranged evenly in spirals, which can be traced around each spike. They should not be spaced too far apart, giving the effect of a birdcage, nor should they be too closely packed. Ideally, they should be almost but not quite touching so that individual florets can be admired whilst the effect of a spike, which is fully furnished with florets, is maintained.

Florets should face the front squarely, although if they face marginally upwards ('proud') this is usually acceptable. However, if florets hang their heads and face downwards ('shy') this is considered to be a major fault.

Florets

There are many variations of form in delphinium florets. They can be single, semi-double or double. The single florets, those with only one row of sepals, should be rejected because they shatter, or drop off the flower early. A good cultivar should retain the sepals on the bottom florets, until the top ones come into flower.

Individual florets should be regular in shape, with clearly defined clusters of eye petals at their centres. The eye petals, or their colour, should not splash out across, or into, the outer sepals. This is especially important in the case of exhibition cultivars. Certain colour combinations such as white or blue florets, with dark eyes, are prone to this, which is considered a major fault.

The florets should ideally be flat rather than cup shaped, so as to shed rainwater efficiently. But, even if they are very slightly cupped, they are still attractive and may be preferred for garden situations where they are possibly less liable to wind damage. It is considered to be a serious fault if the floret is cupped at the top or hooded, or has uneven, irregularly spaced sepals.

Florets should be of good size and at least as big as those of existing named cultivars in the same colour range. Mid-blue cultivars usually produce smaller florets than lighter blue ones. The outer sepals and central eye petals should ideally be thick and substantial, to resist rain and weather damage.

There are many variations in the form of the eye in existing cultivars. Ideally the eye should be regular in shape and form. It should be in a colour that is compatible with, and enhances, that of the floret. However, I have seen eyes that do not conform to the above but still look most attractive. It therefore follows that the combined effect of the floret and eye should be given due consideration. Some cultivars such as 'Tiddles' and 'Pink Ruffles' do not have a distinct eye, but instead have another row of enlarged eye petals the same colour as the outer sepals, giving a double effect. This can be attractive and is certainly acceptable.

Delphinium spikes should be in flower, from top to bottom, before the bottom florets start to shed their sepals. Cultivars such as 'Loch Nevis' and 'Loch Leven' can be seen to have developing seed pods and yet still have retained all their sepals. Certain other cultivars such as 'Rona' and 'Purple Velvet' allow the sepals to die but remain attached to the florets which is not so acceptable. Unless a seedling shows good holding powers it should be discarded.

Colour

"Beauty is in the eye of the beholder" and what is pleasing to one individual is unacceptable to another. Some people like florets bearing two or more colours (or bi-colours), which can be very attractive. Others prefer florets of one pure and even colour only (that is. self-coloured), such as blue, pink or purple. Delphiniums with such florets are generally regarded as preferable, in a flower border, because they have more impact and give a more striking effect. Whatever your preference, colours should be clear, regular and symmetrical around the floret. A wonderful range exists in delphinium cultivars but any colour break into unknown territory is a very big plus. For example, a streaked and veined colouring has been developed recently which the raiser Duncan McGlashan refers to, somewhat prosaically, as 'oddballs'.

The test of time

Although the criteria described give a guide to plant selection, it cannot be emphasised too strongly just how important it is to trial your selected seedlings over several years to test for latent defects. Seedlings usually display a particularly vigorous youth, but this can disappear quickly and at an alarming rate over the next few years. I had a white seedling, which looked absolutely stunning in the first year, and was an exceptionally strong plant. The second year it was less vigorous and the decline was exponential such that by year five no cutting of it would survive.

Similarly, I had a wonderful black eyed, clear blue, seedling that did retain its hybrid vigour. However, at year three the black eye splashed on a few of the florets. During the fourth and fifth years, every single floret splashed. Hence the plant was discarded.

Other undesirable characteristics may be seen to creep in. One needs to test the vulnerability of a plant to producing malformed spikes, or to fasciate, as well as resistance to diseases such as mildew.

It need not always be bad news. Some cultivars can improve in their early years, which can turn a good seedling into a great one. Tom Cowan always used to tell the story as to how 'Loch Leven' underwent this metamorphosis and became one of the greatest ever delphinium introductions. The late Jack Harkness with his rose breeding programme always gave his first year seedling selections a mark out of ten. He too, noted that the seedlings, which finally became marketed as new rose cultivars, had usually scored eight out of ten at first selection whereas those that scored ten ultimately were discarded.

If after five years trial your seedling is still vigorous, devoid of latent defects and distinct enough to differentiate it from any existing cultivar, it should be named and made available so that other delphinium enthusiasts may too enjoy its beauty.

Naming delphiniums

There is no law against anyone naming one of their own prized seedlings. However, it is better by far to register the name with the International Delphinium Register, held by the Royal Horticultural Society, because it will be universally acknowledged as your delphinium's name. Raisers and introducers of new delphiniums are urged to ensure that the names of all their plants have been registered. Forms can be obtained from The International Delphinium Registrar, Royal Horticultural Society's Garden, Wisley, Woking, Surrey, GU23 6QB. There is no fee for basic registration. Nor for a certificate if this is requested.

Your choice of name may need some thinking about because the register has been in operation for many, many years and there can be no duplications. The Registrar will notify you whether the chosen name is acceptable. He is not interested in the quality of your plant. Many delphiniums have been named and have never made the grade in people's gardens. The one sure way to assess the worth of a delphinium is to have it compared against other named cultivars by independent judges.

The R.H.S. delphinium trials

The Royal Horticultural Society holds a yearly trial of delphiniums in their gardens at Wisley. This consists of approximately 90 different cultivars. Each summer a Joint Committee, consisting of Royal Horticultural Society members and Delphinium Society members, assess the plants to select cultivars for an Award of Garden Merit (AGM). The trial has 2 plants of each of these AGM delphiniums as well as 3 each of the newer cultivars that have not received awards. The committee also selects cultivars that are suitable for exhibition, and makes relevant awards. These are a First Class Certificate (FCC) given to plants of outstanding excellence for exhibition; an Award of Merit (AM) given to plants which are of great merit for exhibition and finally a Certificate of Preliminary Commendation (PC) given to a new plant of promise for exhibition. The Joint Committee is also responsible for making a Delphinium Society award, the 'Stuart Ogg Medal', which is given each year to the best delphinium plant growing in the trial.

Anyone may apply to have their plants included in the trial. There is no requirement to be a member of the Royal Horticultural Society or the Delphinium Society. Forms may be obtained from the Secretary of the Royal Horticultural Society. These will ask if the plant is suitable for exhibition or garden decoration. The joint Committee will need to see 3 spikes of the cultivar to pre-assess its worthiness. This will mean that it does need to be an improvement on, or different from, any existing cultivar. If accepted, the raiser will need to provide at least 5 plants the following year. Three will be used in the Trial while the others will be used as stock plants. Finally it should be pointed out that if a plant is to receive an Award of Garden Merit, it should be available to the general gardening public.

Possibly this all sounds a bit complicated but, like many things in life, once the first step is taken the path becomes easier. One thing is sure, that growing your own beautiful delphinium and receiving recognition for your work will be an unforgettable experience.

CHAPTER THIRTEEN

NAMED ELATUM DELPHINIUM CULTIVARS

Compiled by Patrick Booth

The problem with producing a list of plants is always that it will gradually become dated. That is because new and desirable cultivars become available, whilst some of the older ones will deteriorate. There is, of course, no obvious way to avoid the problem. The best way to be kept fully informed about new cultivars is to belong to The Delphinium Society.

All of the named delphinium plants that we include, in this list, will have been propagated vegetatively. That is to say by means of cuttings or (occasionally) micro-propagation. All plants of a particular clone, which we now call a 'cultivar', meaning a cultivated variety, should, therefore be identical with all other plants having the same name. These named cultivars are the best delphiniums obtainable, anywhere.

There is a practice in the nursery trade of selling so called 'Named Plants' that have been grown from seed, usually 'Giant Pacific' strains that may flower true to colour but will be of poor quality and lack perenniality. In our view, the way in which these plants are marketed is misleading, since purchasers confuse them with named cultivars that have been grown from cuttings. Purchasing them is likely to result in disappointment, even if you grow them well! Just so that you know which plants to avoid, we provide a list:

Galahad	~	White with white eyes
Percival	~	White with black eyes
Lancelot	~	Mauve with fawn eyes
Guinevere	~	Rosy lavender with white eyes
Cameliard	~	Bi-coloured lavender with white eyes
King Arthur	~	Purple with white eyes
Black Knight	~	Purple with black eyes
Summer Skies	~	Light blue with creamy yellow eyes
Blue Bird	~	Mid blue with dark eyes
Blue Jay	~	Dark blue with black eyes
Astolat	~	Magenta pinks with black, brown or fawn eyes
Elaine	~	Light magenta pinks with light coloured eyes.

Useful Royal Horticultural Society publications include 'The Plant Finder', in which lists of plants are cross-referenced to the nurseries that supply them. It is updated each year and lists delphinium species in heavy italic type. Named cultivars are shown in ordinary type. Plants grown from 'Giant Pacific', 'Blue Fountain' and other seed strains are also listed in normal type. This is confusing even though their seedling origins may be indicated by the word 'group', or 'series'. The real problem is that the compilers are dependent on the information supplied to them, so that it may not be clear whether the plants are grown from seed or cuttings. If you are in any doubt, ask the nursery or supplier to clarify the matter.

The list of named cultivars that follows is fairly comprehensive but it is not practicable to give opinions on all of them. Comment is made on some but please be aware that the performance of individual cultivars can vary from garden to garden.

Plant heights will vary according to position, especially if grown in shade, general growing conditions and standard of cultivation. Typically, delphiniums grow to 1.5mtrs or 5'0" tall. That will be the normal height of all the plants listed, unless stated to the contrary. Most of the delphiniums listed below have semi-double florets, with more than one row of petals surrounding a central eye or 'bee'. They will flower mid-season unless they are specifically stated to be different.

The majority of the plants are available from one or other of the specialist delphinium nurseries. However, some are not available commercially so that the only possible sources are likely to be Delphinium Society members who grow and propagate them.

Blue delphiniums

Everyone expects delphiniums to be blue. The colours of some are exceptionally bright and intense. However, their quality can be problematical. Even the best plants have faults although the colours make them especially desirable. The brightest mid-blue delphinium, having florets with white eyes, is *'Blue Nile'* (AGM 1993) (1.7mtrs or 5'6"). Its colour is unsurpassed but it can be a temperamental grower. It has a somewhat loose flower spike and floret placement is usually uneven. Fasciation can occur even with minimal feeding. It is a plant that, despite its faults is well worth trying. An alternative choice is *'Joan Edwards'*, which has very slightly darker but still bright blue florets, also with white eyes. We think it performs more reliably. *'Kathleen Cooke'* (AGM 1997, PC 1995) is an excellent plant for garden or exhibition, having slightly softer and lighter colouring than the foregoing. Its floret placement is a little tight but it is a reliable show plant. *'Fenella'* (AGM 1993) is a fine plant having bright gentian blue florets. The eye is black, with gold hairs. *'Nicholas Woodfield'* is virtually identical. Among the lighter blue delphiniums, we would single out *'Loch Leven'* (AGM 1993) (1.7mtrs or 5'6") because it is an outstanding plant. The florets can show a pink tinge in some weather conditions, but are well shaped and formed with white eyes. It is vigorous and long-lived. *'Clifford Sky'* (AGM 1999) (1.8mtrs or 6'0") is by no means faultless, but it is strong growing and flowers very late indeed, extending the season. It has exceptionally pure sky blue florets with white eyes. Disadvantages are that it is very tall and has thick, rather soft stems.*'Crown Jewel'* (1.7mtrs or 5'6") (Late) is a good reliable plant that has soft light blue, well-formed florets and with neat dark eyes. *'Lord Butler'* (AGM 1993) (1.4mtrs or 4'6") has Cambridge blue florets with white eyes. It is an excellent shorter growing Delphinium, as is *'Cupid'* (1.2mtrs or 4'0"), having pale sky blue florets with white eyes. *'Galileo'* (PC 1999) (1.7mtrs or 5'6") is a recent introduction that appears very fine. It is mid-blue with violet overtones towards the edges of the petals, with a pink flush towards the centres and dark eyes.

Other blue Delphiniums, worth considering are:

'Anne Kenrick' (Pale blue/white eye)

'Blue Dawn' (AGM 1993) (1.7mtrs or 5'6") (Late) (Light blue/brown eye)

'Blue Jade' (1.2mtrs or 4'0") (Light blue/brown eye)

'Blue Lagoon' (1.7mtrs or 5'6") (Mid-blue/white eye, blue fleck)

'Blue Oasis' (1.2mtrs or 4'0") (Pastel blue/light brown eye)

'Cristella' (Early) (Mid blue/white eye)

'Dora Larkan' (1.7 mtrs or 5'6") (Light blue/white eye)

'Graham Robert' (1.2 mtrs or 4'0") (Gentian blue/white eye)

'Kestrel' (Very early) (Dark blue/dark eye)

'Leonora' (Mid blue/white eye)

'Loch Nevis' (1.8mtrs or 6'0") (Late) (Mid blue/white eye)

'Loch Katrine' (Dark blue/dark eye)

'Molly Buchanan' (1.7 mtrs or 5'6") (Gentian blue/black and gold eye)

'Pericles' (Late) (Sky blue/white eye)

'Pandora' (PC 1999) (1.7mtrs or 5'6") (Mid blue/black eye striped blue)

'Sabrina' (1.1mtrs or 3'6") (Mid blue/white eye)

'Shimmer' (1.7mtrs or 5'6") (Late) (Mid blue/white eye)

'Skyline' (Late) (Sky blue/white with double effect)

'Thamesmead' (AGM 1996) (Dark blue/dark eye)

'Walton Benjamin' (Mid blue plus black eye)

Lavender and mauve delphiniums

'Emily Hawkins' (AGM 1993) (1.75mtrs or 5'9") is an exceptionally fine plant having beautifully formed florets in lavender mauve, with a contrasting fawn eye. The florets are well and evenly spaced on the spike. It throws many shoots in the spring and so needs more thinning than most. A good, reliable plant that is tough, grows well and looks good. Definitely a 'must have'. 'Min' (AGM 1994, AM 1996, Stuart Ogg medal 1993) (1.7mtrs or 5'6") is equally fine, having good well-placed florets veined in lavender and with neat dark eyes. 'Conspicuous' (AGM 1993, AM 1996) (1.7mtrs or 5'6") has very nice light mauve-blue florets with dark brown eyes. It is an older cultivar that has proved its worth over the years. 'Anne Woodfield' has silvery florets flushed blue. It grows well and seems vigorous; a good garden plant. 'Gillian Dallas' (AGM 1993, PC 1994, Stuart Ogg medal 1990) (Late) is bluish mauve with white eyes and is a very attractive plant, suitable for show bench or garden. 'Mighty Atom' (AGM 1996) (1.4mtrs or 4'6") (Late) is pure lavender. It wins the prize for a big spike on a short plant, flowering from 0.6 mtrs (2'0") above ground level. Don't overfeed as it makes the plant look coarse, but it is a very desirable, long-lived plant. 'Walton Gemstone' (AGM 1996, PC 2000) (1.7mtrs or 5'6") has very pleasing and nicely shaped florets of very pale lilac with white eyes. 'Tiger eye' (PC 2001) is a recent introduction having pure mauve florets with prominent black and gold eyes. It is very attractive and a fine plant.

Other lavender or mauve Delphiniums worth considering are:

'Alice Artindale' (1.7mtrs or 5'6") (Mauve double florets)

'Baby Doll' (1.2mtrs or 4'0") (Pale mauve)

'Can Can' (AGM 1999) (1.4mtrs or 4'6") (Pinky mauve striped double)

'Cher' (Late) (Silvery mauve and amethyst picotee)

'Dolly Bird' (Pale mauve/white eye)
'Gemma' (Lavender/white eye)
'Gordon Forsyth' (AM 1994) (1.7 mtrs or 5'6") (Late) (Amethyst/dark eye)
'Fanfare' (AGM 1993, AM 1996) (1.7mtrs or 5'6") (Early) (Silvery mauve/white eye)
'Franjo Sahin' (Mauve picotee, pale centre and dark eye)
'Florestan' (Lavender/prominent dark eye)
'Giotto' (AGM 1993, AM 1995) (Mauve with blue overlay/fawn eye)
'Michael Ayres' (AGM 1998, AM 1995) (1.8mtrs or 6'0") (Mauve)
'Mystique' (1.7mtrs or 5'6") (Silvery mauve shaded blue/white eye)
'Oliver' (AGM 1998) (Mauve shaded blue/black eye)
'Royal Wedding' (1.7mtrs or 5'6") (Late) (Mauve shades/white eye)
'Tiddles' (AGM 1993) (1.7mtrs or 5'6") (Lavender/double)
'Vanessa Mae' (Violet blue/dark brown eye)
'Vespers' (1.7mtrs or 5'6") (Mauve shaded blue/white eye)
'Walton Beauty' (Violet/white eye)

Pink delphiniums

Strictly speaking the colours of the pink elatum hybrids embrace a range of magentas. They all have a tendency to fade in hot weather. The best of the pinks are good vigorous garden plants, despite having red Californian species in their ancestry. The darkest coloured plant is 'Lucia Sahin' (AGM 2001, AM 1996) (1.7mtrs or 5'6"). This has well formed florets, with dark eyes, set out on a good spike. The colour alone would make it a must. It is, however a recent introduction and is in short supply. 'Rosemary Brock' (AGM 1993, AM 1995, Stuart Ogg Medal 1995) is at least as recommendable, for show or the garden. It has good dusky magenta pink florets with brown eyes. They are evenly spaced on well-shaped spikes. The plant is vigorous. 'Our Deb' (AGM 1996) (1.7mtrs or 5'6") has paler florets with dark eyes. 'Claire' (AGM 1998) also has pale pink florets with fawn eyes that look most attractive. It is a good garden plant. 'Royal Flush' (also called 'Langdons Royal Flush') (AGM 1993) is an excellent plant with pink florets and white eyes. 'Summerfield Miranda' (AGM 1993, PC 1995) is an attractive pale pink with brown eyes. 'Darling Sue' (Early) has very attractive pale pink florets, with darker veining and a brown eye. 'Blackberry Ice' has purplish veining, which overlies a white floret with pink flush. It has a brown eye and is a recent introduction.

Other good pink Delphiniums include:
'Cherub' (AGM 2001) (Late) (Pink tinged mauve/white eye)
'Clifford Lass' (Dusky pink/black eye)
'Clifford Pink' (1.7mtrs or 5'6") (Deep pink/cream eye)
'Cymbeline' (1.7mtrs or 5'6") (Deep pink)
'Garden Party' (Pale pink/white eye)
'Pink Ruffles' (Pale pink/double flowers)
'Ruby' (Mulberry pink/brown eye)
'Strawberry Fair' (1.7mtrs or 5'6") (Mulberry rose/white eye)
'Summerfield Diana' (Late) (Pale pink/brown eye)
'Titania' (Pink with pink and white striped eye)
'Turkish Delight' (1.7mtrs or 5'6") (Pale pink/white eye)

Purple and indigo delphiniums

Purple and indigo (by which we mean the dark, purplish blue colours) are usually strong growing plants, with large thickly textured florets. Many are prone to mildew so that spraying with fungicides, occasionally, is desirable. Purple coloured Delphiniums vary in terms of brightness and intensity. The brightest of all must be 'Chelsea Star' (1.7mtrs or 5'6"). The rich purple florets are each well formed with a white eye. The spikes are, however, a bit loose. Floret placement is also uneven and the plant suffers badly from mildew. It is also not very perennial. 'Summerfield Oberon' (AM 1990) is a recent introduction having similar colouring. Some dislike it because the spikes are carried some way above the foliage. However, its floret placement is better and the plant looks superior. 'Purple Velvet' is a good plant, having deep purple florets with black eyes. 'Bruce' (AGM 1993, Stuart Ogg medal 1986) (1.8mtrs or 6'0") has slate-purple florets and a greyish brown eye. It looks rather sombre but is an outstanding plant for garden or exhibition. It throws a multitude of shoots that must be thinned out, each spring. 'Faust' (AGM 1993) (1.8mtrs or 6'0") is an old cultivar that has rather untidy florets, uniquely coloured in ultramarine blue and plum shades, with dark eyes. It is vigorous and reliable. 'Blue Tit' (1.2mtrs or 4'0") (Early) (Dark indigo blue/black eye) is a tough, shorter growing delphinium of some age. Since it has no Giant Pacific blood, it is a valuable resource for plant breeders.

Other purple delphiniums that are worthwhile, include:

'Cassius' (AGM 1996) (1.7mtrs or 5'6") (Late) (Purplish blue/dark eye)
'Eamonn Andrews' (Light purple-pink/white eye)
'Nimrod' (2mtrs or 6'6") (Purple/white eye)
'Nobility' (Purple shaded blue/dark eye)
'Purple Ruffles' (1.7mtrs or 5'6") (Purple/double flowered)
'Thundercloud' (1.7mtrs or 5'6") (Deep purple/black eye)

White delphiniums

Some white Delphiniums are whiter than others. Many growers have a particular fondness for those with dark eyes. Of those, the standard recommendation would be 'Sandpiper' (AGM 1993, Stuart Ogg medal 1992). This is an early flowering cultivar with a slight creamy tinge to its petals and has a dark brown eye. The florets are well formed with good placement, not too loose or too close. The spikes are pyramidal. It is a good plant for the garden as well as exhibition. 'Atholl' (AGM 2000) (Early) is, we think, equally fine. Its petals are very white and it has a neat black eye. The florets are good, if a little loosely spaced on a slightly pyramidal spike. The spikes seem to last well and retain their freshness, even in poor weather. 'Lilian Bassett' (AGM 1995) (1.4 mtrs or 4'6") is a recent shorter growing introduction, also white florets with black eyes, that has performed very well in the Delphinium trials and is well furnished with laterals. 'Constance Rivett' (AGM 1998) (1.2mtrs or 4'0") is another recent introduction. It has well formed white florets, with a white eye. It is a desirable short growing plant for the smaller garden, or front of border. 'Jill Curley', is a taller growing alternative. 'Rona' (Early) has a somewhat narrow spike, nice greeny-white florets with white eye whilst a new introduction, 'Summerfield Ariane' (Very early) has a green tinged white eye. 'Olive Poppleton' (AGM 2000, Stuart Ogg medal 1982) (1.7mtrs or 5'6") (Early) is an established cultivar with an unusual fawn eye. It is well worth growing, but has a fault in that the petals on the bottom florets start to drop well before the top of the spike comes into flower. *'Elizabeth Cook'* (AGM 2000) (White with white eye) is a recent introduction that promises to be good.

Other white delphiniums, worth consideration, include:

'Moonbeam' (White/white eye)
'Silver Jubilee' (1.7mtrs or 5'6") (White/Black eye)
'White Ruffles' (White) (Double)

Cream and yellow delphiniums

Cream and yellow flowered delphiniums always have ochre tinged leaves, and stems, that are not diseased but are certainly unattractive. They should never be placed in a front of border position for that reason. Why then, you will ask, grow plants with funny looking leaves. We think that the answer is that the creams do 'set off' the other Delphinium colours. Although there are some named delphiniums that look yellow, they actually have deep cream petals, with yellow eyes. *'Sunkissed'* (AGM 2000, PC 1997) is a recent introduction and therefore relatively untested. However, we are certain that it is the best cream with yellow eyes. *'Celebration'* has cream florets with a dark brown eye. The plant has relatively short spikes.

Other cream Delphiniums that are worthwhile include:

'Butterball' (Cream with yellow eyes)
'Sungleam' (AGM 1993, Stuart Ogg medal 1984) (Cream with yellow eye)

Green flowered and tinted delphiniums

There is only one pure green flowered delphinium, which is *'Dunsden Green'*, which is semi-double but has no eye. It is a recent cultivar and there has been insufficient time to assess its merits. *'Spindrift'* (AGM1994, Stuart Ogg medal 1986) is predominantly mauve with blue overtones. It develops a green/turquoise colour, to a degree that varies with weather and soil conditions. *'Gossamer'* is similar but paler in colour. Both plants are beautiful. *'Susan Edmunds'* is a recently introduced shorter growing plant. It has greenish mauve striped narrow petals and is fully double — definitely one for the flower arrangers.

Suitable delphiniums for exhibition

It is fortunate that many delphinium cultivars do not deteriorate rapidly in their vigour or constitution. Providing a good stock is maintained, there are several that will be suitable for exhibiting over many years. There are some that have proved their worth for well in excess of a decade and show no sign of losing the ability to win prizes. The following cultivars can be recommended for consistently good exhibition results:

'Beryl Burton'	~	Deep purplish red which qualifies as a dark cultivar.
'Bruce'	~	Slate/violet colour which qualifies as a dark cultivar.
'Emily Hawkins'	~	Mauve with fawn eye.
'Gillian Dallas'	~	Heliotrope.
'Gordon Forsyth'	~	Deep lavender.
'Lucia Sahin'	~	Deep reddish purple which qualifies as a dark cultivar.
'Min'	~	Pale lavender.
'Rosemary Brock'	~	Magenta pink.

'Sandpiper'   ~ White with brown eye.
'Summerfield Diana'   ~ Pale mauve/pink.
'Summerfield Miranda' ~ Light magenta pink.
'Walton Gemstone'   ~ Pale slate.

There are other delphiniums with suitable qualities for exhibiting and there will continue to be more available from leading hybridisers to take the place of those cultivars that deteriorate and fail to meet the required standards.

Plant collections

The National Council for Conservation of Plants and Gardens (The NCCPG) is an organisation that aims to conserve and protect our heritage of garden plants. There are two National collections of delphinium held under its auspices.

The first National Collection is held by Leeds City Council and is located at Temple Newsam Park, Temple Newsam Rd., Leeds, LS15 OAD.

The second National collection is held by 'Rougham Hall Nurseries', A14, Rougham, Bury St Edmunds, Suffolk, IP30 9LZ.

Specialist delphinium nurseries

The Nurseries and Nurserymen, listed below, are specialists in the propagation and growing of delphiniums:

Blackmore and Langdon Ltd: Pensford, Bristol, BS39 4JL. Tel: 01275 332300
This Nursery was founded in 1901. Since then, it has specialised in delphiniums. Using a combination of careful line breeding and rigorous selection, a stream of ever improving plants was produced by them, until the 1970's when large-scale breeding ceased. The nursery includes modern, amateur raised, plants in its lists. Blackmore and Langdon remain as the premier specialist delphinium nursery to this day. Other specialities include border phlox, begonia and gloxinia. They also do a nice line in aquilegia and polyanthus seeds from their own strains.

'Woodfields', 'Wood End', Clifford Chambers, Stratford-on-Avon, Warwickshire, CV37 6HR.
This is a small but professionally run nursery which lists a good selection of modern delphinium cultivars including some raised at the nursery as well as others by amateur growers. The nursery is also well known for carnations and 'New generation lupins', which have been awarded a succession of R.H.S. gold medals at Chelsea flower show.

Rougham Hall Nurseries: A14, Rougham, Bury St Edmunds, Suffolk, IP30 9LZ.
Tel: 01359 270577 Fax: 01359 271149 Email: kelvin-harbutt@msn.com
This nursery has a good selection of recommendable hybrid elatum delphinium cultivars for sale. In addition, it lists a selection of bushy 'Belladonna' cultivars. The nursery specialises also in Iceland poppies and has a large selection of hardy perennial plants for sale.

John Barrington, Newport Mills Nursery, Wrantage, Taunton, Somerset, TA3 6DJ.
Tel: 01823 490231 Mobile 07950 035668
John Barrington is a farmer but also runs a small specialist nursery. He has a truly comprehensive list of delphinium cultivars, so that if you are really stuck for obtaining a particular plant, he may be able to help. John Barrington has, for a number of years, supplied the plants that are used on the Delphinium Society stands at Chelsea. The displays always attract admiring comments.

'Emily Hawkins': Raised and introduced by David and Shirley Bassett. This is an outstanding delphinium, both for garden display and for exhibition. The combination of mauve florets and fawn eyes is unusual and attractive.

'Graham Robert': This is a short growing delphinium, raised and introduced by Jim Cook. It has exceptionally bright mid-blue florets with white eyes and is an exceptionally dainty plant.

'Bruce': This plant was raised and introduced by Duncan McGlashan. The slatey mauve florets are very large. This cultivar grows well in the garden, being vigorous and long-lived. It is also a good exhibition plant.

'Sunkissed': Raised by Nigel Moody, this plant is generally acknowledged as being the best cream delphinium.

'Clifford Lass': Raised at the Woodfield's nursery, near Stratford-on-Avon, this has attractive paler pink florets. The dark brown eyes are a nice contrast.

'Emily Hawkins'

'Graham Robert'

'Bruce'

'Sunkissed'

'Clifford Lass'

CHAPTER FOURTEEN

GROWING SPECIES DELPHINIUMS IN THE GARDEN

By Shirley Bassett

The wide range of colours offered by delphiniums currently grown in gardens is such that many people do not attempt to grow any *Delphinium* species. A pity, because among the array of *Delphinium* species are plants with a variety of architecture and leaf form, flowering over a range of months and in colours from the whole spectrum, brilliant blues, yellow and red. Despite these useful features, seeds of many species are often difficult to locate in catalogues. In part, this could be due to limited demand by customers who may be inhibited by their past failures. The absence of detailed information on germination and growing requirements, coupled with low seed viability due to problems of collection and incorrect storage, can discourage the most enthusiastic grower. Many *Delphinium* species are not difficult to grow, providing one tries to understand their normal habitat. Natural selection has resulted in adaptation to survive the rigours of weather and environments that may differ greatly from the conditions in our own gardens.

Many delphiniums are found in mountainous areas, often in rather poor soils and under snow cover for many months of the year. The leaves, flowers and seeds may be produced in a relatively short time after the snow has melted and before high temperatures and/or lack of moisture induce dormancy. Plants of some species may take several years to build up to a sufficient size to flower. In warmer areas of the world, annuals and biennials are found, although many annuals are no longer placed in the genus *Delphinium* but are separated into the genus *Consolida*.

All *Delphinium* species possess five, coloured, sepals with the upper sepal extended into a spur of variable length. Petals, four in number, are coloured and the upper pair are prolonged into nectaries which are inserted into the spur and may be termed 'honey leaves' or the 'eye'. The form of the flower has given rise to the common name 'larkspur'. Wild delphiniums are often called larkspurs in their natural environments. A further important characteristic is the possession of between three to five carpels (i.e. seed pods) producing numerous seeds.

It is probably most rewarding to start by growing those species which are least demanding and from seed that is readily available. One can then move on to a larger number of species, which are not difficult but require a little more attention to meet their needs. Finally, when one has gained that ill-defined practical ability (delphinium 'green-fingers' perhaps?), one can tackle those more challenging species.

Among the first category are the two red species, *D. cardinale* and *D. nudicaule*, the brilliant blue dwarf *D. grandiflorum* var. *chinense* and *D. tatsienense* which may be available in blue and white forms. *D. nudicaule*, flowering on short stems devoid of leaves, produces a few cupped orange-red florets and is an ideal plant for the rockery. The tall-growing *D. cardinale* produces a stiff-stemmed spike of well-separated florets and numerous laterals in colours which range from bright scarlet, orange, apricot and also a less common yellow variant. In its native California, *D. cardinale* grows through other shrubs, termed chaparral, which support its tall stems arising from a narrow base and tuberous rootstock. Plants must therefore be adequately supported in the garden. *D. grandiflorum* var. *chinense* and the true *D. tatsienense*, which is less common, have heavily-dissected foliage and produce flowers on two or three branching spikes. The brilliant blue of the form 'Blue Butterfly' and the paler blue form 'Sky Blue' together with a variant 'Blue Mirror', which is bright gentian blue and lacks the characteristic spur, make an ideal edge to any border. Although generally grown as half-hardy annuals, they are perennials and will survive providing the soil is well drained during the winter months.

All of these species will germinate readily in good compost from a spring sowing, as early as your ability to provide light for the seedlings allows, since germination temperatures required are relatively low, 15°C (60°F). I prefer to allow germination to occur on wet kitchen towel in a small, lidded container, since each germinating seed can be transferred individually to just below the surface of compost in a small 5 cm (2") pot thus eliminating the need for pricking out. Although these species will tolerate root disturbance, many of the less easy ones will not and this is a source of failure, so it is worth learning the technique at the beginning. When growing these species, a noticeable feature of *D. nudicaule* is that the first true leaves arise from below ground, in contrast to the other species where the leaves appear from a point between the two cotyledons (seed leaves).

Another species that germinates readily and produces plants of a very different form is *D. ceratophorum* from China. The hairy leaves, reminiscent of a buttercup, are produced on spreading stems. The flowers, produced on stiff horizontal growths, are dark violet; with a darker eye and with a long down-curving spur. Thus it requires plenty of space at the front of a border to spread around. Also requiring ample space is the biennial, *D. requienii* from the Mediterranean. The relatively large seeds (3 mm or 0.1") germinate readily and produce two broad, veined cotyledons. The first glossy leaves appear about three weeks later. *D. requienii* is best started later in the year, May to July so plants in their first summer produce leaves only and rarely a flower spike. These leaves do not disappear during the winter months and the plants, although reasonably hardy, appear vulnerable to rotting of the stem at the soil surface due to excess water or heavy winter snow. Providing the plants survive the winter, they grow steadily during the spring reaching a massive circumference and producing a substantial main spike with large numbers of laterals. The flowers are small, blue-grey in colour with prominent purple anthers, resembling miniature orchids. A major attraction to pollinating insects; flowers are followed by hairy seedpods producing large numbers of seeds. It is a superb plant to fill a gap but has a horrid smell when the leaves are brushed and, in common with other delphiniums, poisonous seeds.

It is worth looking for seeds of annual delphiniums as they are rewarding to grow. *D. balcanicum*, from the Eastern Mediterranean, produces plants around 0.9 mtrs (3'0") in height with multi-branching stems bearing numerous florets in deep purplish blue. Although the individual flowers are very small, the overall impression is a mass of colour in late summer. The continuous branching nature of the growth ensures colour over a long time period.

Species, which require more attention to their needs, include some from North America, Europe and Asia. Their seeds share a common feature, requiring a period of at least four weeks continuous cold/wet treatment (4°C or 40°F) before they will germinate. Clearly pans of seeds in compost can be left outside during the winter months but are vulnerable to pests, e.g. mice, and to the vagaries of the climate, especially in areas where the winter temperature is rarely low enough for long periods. To overcome these problems it is better to use a refrigerator and to place the seeds on wet kitchen towel, in lidded containers, checking for germination towards the end of the time period.

Among the North American species in this group are *D. hansenii* and *D. hesperium,* both with long flowering spikes (0.6 to 0.9 metres, or 2'0" to 3'0"), many laterals and a number of colour forms. These two delphiniums occur only in California and produce a rosette of leaves at the base of the plant, which in *D. hansenii* are marked with spots of chocolate colour when newly produced. The flowering spikes of this delphinium carry up to 25 florets in dark purplish blue but can also be found with pink or white flowers. *D. hesperium* generally produces larger and more numerous florets in blue, while in the subspecies *pallescens,* a much smaller number of florets in white, pale lavender or pink are found. In both these species the appearance of the flowering spike is accompanied by the loss of the basal leaves, a disconcerting habit! After seed production these plants become dormant and must remain dry until the next flowering season. Since it is often difficult to ensure that these conditions are found in the open garden, it is a good idea to grow these plants in large pots (4 litre), and keep them under cover. Watering these containers in early spring is followed by a dramatic reappearance of the plants. Another Californian species, which requires drier conditions especially after flowering, is *D. parryi,* ideal for a rock garden site. Around 0.5 metres tall (18"), the flower spike carries relatively large florets in dark blue, which are spreading in form while in a subspecies *purpureum,* the deep purple sepals are reflexed. This species also loses basal leaves on flowering.

D. trolliifolium is widely distributed in Northern California, the Columbia River Valley and the Willamette Valley in Oregon. This tall growing species thrives under wetter conditions and produces deep blue florets with dramatic white eyes in the spring, from April into early June. The flower spike is more pyramidal than in any of the preceding species, but requires support during the growing period. Although not flowering in the first year of growth when seedlings may not even grow true leaves, it does appear to be quite long lived, at least under our growing conditions near Bath.

Across the world in Asia, there are delphiniums which may be closely related to ancestral types, namely *D. brunonianum* and *D. cashmerianum* from the Himalayan region. These species possess flowers in which the characteristic spur is reduced and bulbous sepals in violet-blue enclose the stamens giving a hooded appearance. Seedlings remain small during their first summer, die down and reappear to grow to flowering size the following year. After flowering the plants become dormant and require dry conditions. A more typical species, *D. pylzowii* from China has dissected foliage and violet-blue florets arranged on short spikes. It is an attractive dwarf delphinium for the rock garden, but appears to be very short lived, about three years, under our conditions.

The beautiful yellow *D. semibarbatum* (previously called, and widely known as, *D. zalil*) comes from Iran and Afghanistan. The plant has very thin, divided leaves and produces wiry spikes bearing numerous florets in shades of colour ranging from a pale lemon to a bright yellow. Perhaps surprisingly, the small grey scaly seeds require three weeks cold/wet treatment before germinating. The seedlings resent transplanting and care is needed at this stage; use of individual pots for the germinating seed is preferable for this species. Unless germination occurs early in the year, seedlings fail to reach flowering size before summer dormancy sets in. It is important to keep plants in continuous growth by adequate water supply since hot dry conditions lead to yellowing of the leaves and dormancy. Plants in containers can be kept dry during the winter months and reawakened by watering in the spring. Again it is more difficult to maintain conditions of drought in the garden but ground at the base of a wall can provide a suitable habitat.

There are many more species of *Delphinium* that require this modest length of cold/wet treatment before they will germinate, that is around four weeks, but the major difficulty is the acquisition of seed. Even if seed is available, the flowers are often too small or the flowering spike too unimpressive for use in the garden. European species such as *D. caucasicum* and *D. przewaldski* are relatively easy to grow and both produce narrow spikes with small florets, the former with blue sepals and white petals, the latter violet with a black eye. A widely distributed North American species known variously as the prairie or white larkspur, *D. carolinianum* (formerly *D. virescens*) produces a spike with a number of white florets. These have an extremely hairy appearance due to 'beards', numerous long hairs on the lower petals. This plant grows in dry grassy plains, fields and roadsides in Colorado, parts of Arizona, Kansas, and into Wisconsin and Illinois. Obviously this plant demands a dry situation to succeed. A very different plant, both in its requirements for moist, gravel soil and in its appearance is *D. uliginosum*. Found only in parts of California, it is a very distinctive species producing basal leaves which are fleshy and three-lobed, fan-shaped in outline: quite unlike those of any other delphinium. A short spike, bearing a large number of deep blue-purple florets and lacking any leaves, is produced in late May to June.

Species, which appear to be more challenging, are those in which the germination time is lengthy, and the conditions required to obtain successful flowering are less easy to achieve, especially in the open garden. Into this category come species from North America, some widely distributed through mountainous regions of Oregon, Washington into California and east to Montana and Colorado, while others may be more limited in their distribution. They include *D. barbeyi, D. bicolor, D. burkei, D. geyeri, D. multiplex, D. nelsoni, D. nuttallianum, D. occidentale* and *D. viridescens*. Seeds of the majority of these species appear to require at least three months cold/wet treatment in the refrigerator and some, like *D. geyeri*, need two such periods before germination. Clearly in their natural habitat, seeds from these plants must remain dormant during the long periods of snow cover that they normally experience. Even after germination, the seedlings are not easy to grow on, often only producing a pair of cotyledons at the summit of a single stalk in the first season! Patience, together with the correct moisture level is required during the summer and subsequent months, before growth resumes in the early spring. In order to obtain seedlings of sufficient maturity to survive through this dormancy period, it is advisable to commence the period of cold/wet treatment as early as November to ensure germination in early spring. During this period, containers should be checked periodically for adequate moisture, since they can dry out, resulting in death of the valuable seed.

The majority of these American species flower in shades of blue, generally dark blue to purple-blue, with a variety of flower form and plant height. However, *D. viridescens* is an unusual plant with deeply dissected lower leaves in drab yellow-green and a spike of cup-shaped greenish-yellow florets, sometimes with purplish streaks. Living in wet, stream side meadows, it is not easy to please.

In conclusion, some general points are worth noting. It is better not to use all your seed at once, storing any surplus seed dry in the refrigerator. Try a number of different germination regimes, and grow your seedlings in small individual containers to avoid root disturbance at transplanting. Never throw a pot away if a seedling apparently dies and disappears, but keep dry until the seasons change. Many of these delphinium species are extremely susceptible to mildew and to infestations of red spider mites, both outside and under cover. Unless preventative measures are taken, such pests can kill the plants. Do find out all you can about the natural environment of the species you are growing and try to check that the leaves and flowers match the description you have. Finally make some notes on the methods you have used; it is so easy to forget!

When at last you are successful and your delphinium species flowers, enjoy it and perhaps try a little hand-pollination, as seed is in many cases, difficult to come by.

Delphinium trollifolium: An attractive, taller growing species from Northern California and surrounding areas.

Delphinium grandiflorum, var *chinenense:* This is a variable species from China. There are a number of selected seed strains available, which are short growing and floriferous. *Delphinium grandiflorum* may have been one of the species from which the elatum garden hybrids were developed.

Delphinium Belladonna 'Atlantis': Belladonna delphiniums are relatively short growing and have a bushy style of growth. They are repeat flowering and reliable perennial plants. 'Atlantis' is a modern and exceptional cultivar.

Delphinium semibarbatum: Formerly known as *Delphinium zalil,* is a species from Afghanistan and neighbouring countries. It is a beautiful plant but not easy to grow in Britain.

Delphinium cardinale: This is a tall growing Californian species. A number of selected seed strains are available which are of variable form and are best treated as annuals.

Delphinium nudicaule 'Laurin': *Delphinium nudicaule* is a short growing red Californian species. Tuberous rooted, it is a tender perennial but well worth growing in a sheltered rockery or trough, where it should persist for a number of years. The plant shown is three years old.

University hybrid 'Princess Caroline': The University hybrid delphiniums have been bred, basically, by hybridising the red Californian species, *Delphinium cardinale* and *Delphinium nudicaule.* The resulting plants were then crossed with the modern elatum hybrid delphiniums. Considerable further breeding work has been undertaken since but the plants are not reliably perennial in Britain. They are grown, under glass, in Holland for the cut flower trade.

Seedling – University hybrid x elatum cultivar: Raised by Roy Latty, this plant suffered from similar problems as the Univrsity hybrids and was discarded, despite its unusual and attractive florets.

Delphinium trollifolium

Delphinium grandiflorum, var chinenense

Delphinium Belladonna 'Atlantis'

Delphinium semibarbatum

Delphinium Cardinale

Delphinium nudicaule 'Laurin'

University hybrid 'Princess Caroline'

Seedling – University hybrid × Elatum Cultivar

OTHER HYBRID DELPHINIUMS

By Patrick Booth

Belladonna delphiniums

It seems that some very discerning gardeners actually do not like the elatum hybrid delphiniums and consider them to be big fat and ugly. Extraordinary! However, if we all liked the same things, the world would be a more boring place. For those who want something more dainty, there are Belladonna hybrids, which have a generally bushy style of growing. Single florets resemble those of delphinium species, about 50mm (2") across with long spurs. The Belladonnas are generally speaking tough, reliable and perennial garden plants. Their cultural requirements are broadly similar to those for the larger elatum cultivars although, heavy nitrogenous feeding would be inappropriate. It is still sensible to feed, occasionally, with a balanced or high potash fertiliser and pay careful attention to watering. Slugs and snails are as much of a problem, unfortunately, as with the larger cultivars. Belladonna delphiniums are relatively wind resistant, but require support nonetheless. Pea sticks are inconspicuous and, usually, adequate.

There are few Belladonna cultivars, but here is a list of older types:

'Capri'	~	Sky blue ~ Light eye
'Cliveden Beauty'	~	Cambridge blue ~ Light eye ~ Fertile
'Isis'	~	Violet blue ~ Light eye
'Lamartine'	~	Purplish blue ~ Light eye
'Moerheimi'	~	White
'Naples'	~	Gentian blue ~ Light eye
'Orion'	~	Cobalt blue ~ Light eye
'Wendy'	~	Gentian shading to purple

There are some, more modern, Belladonna hybrids originating usually from Germany. Those include:

'Volkerfrieden'	~	Mid blue
'Atlantis'	~	Dark blue
'Balkeid'	~	Soft blue
'Piccolo'	~	Light blue
'Casa Blanca'	~	White (seed strain)

Belladonna Delphiniums are now generally accepted as being a group of plants that have resulted from chance hybridisation between elatum cultivars as one parent and either one of the species *D. grandiflorum* or *D. tatsienense* as another. The plants that result, from crossing elatum garden hybrids (tetraploid with 32 chromosomes) and diploid species (with 16), are triploids having 24 chromosomes, for which reason most Belladonnas are sterile and do not usually set seed. Chromosome doubling can occur spontaneously and it seems that seeds saved when this occurs can be grown on. The resulting plants should be fertile hexaploids with 48 chromosomes. Therefore, if Belladonna delphiniums do set seeds, those may be worth growing.

Connecticut Yankee delphiniums

Edward Steichen trained as an artist, became one of the greatest photographers of the twentieth century and was also a great horticulturalist. He is remembered as the breeder of 'Connecticut Yankee' delphiniums: a seed strain from which bushy garden hybrids, fairly similar in habit but superior to the Belladonna hybrids, could be grown. Their main drawback, in Britain at least, has been suggestions that they are short lived. Their origin is understood to have been a cross, made between a Belladonna type garden hybrid and the species *D. tatsienense*. Further breeding was undertaken that involved other species, including *D. cashmerianum* and *D. elatum*. The result was a sterile hybrid, which was described by Steichen as elatum/belladonna/tatsienense. This was chemically treated to induce doubling of the chromosomes to produce a race of fertile hybrids that are assumed to be hexaploids with 48 chromosomes. The plants grow about 0.9 mtrs (3'0") tall and have single flowers up to 90mm (3.5") across, in a variety of blue, white and purple shades. 'Connecticut Yankee' seeds are still available but plants grown from them will vary considerably, depending on their source. Basically, as with the 'Giant Pacific' seed strains, good breeding procedures have been neglected so that the plants are not as desirable as they once were. Nevertheless, they remain compact growing and do not grow taller in their second and subsequent years, which can be a problem with some Belladonnas. They are also very effective plants for large pots. The 'Connecticut Yankee' seed strains seem to be available from very few seed merchants and, clearly, will not be available for long if nothing is done. They have the advantage of being fertile; setting seeds readily with the result that there is good potential for breeding, if anyone would like to take that on as a project.

Red or pink delphiniums and 'University hybrids'

Hybridists are always trying to breed something different. Sometimes, the results of their work seem to be questionable. It may be right to be cautious about such things as split corona daffodils, which forsake the beautiful and unique trumpet form of their forebears. But, many plants benefit from a wider colour range.

American and Dutch breeders have been fascinated with the two red Californian delphinium species, the tall growing *D. cardinale* and the small *D. nudicaule*, both of which have tuberous roots. Their dream has been to incorporate red and pink colours into taller growing garden elatum hybrids. There is a major difficulty, however. Chromosomes are the basic building blocks of reproduction, contained within the male pollen and the female ovaries of plants. They must be compatible, and equal in number, for cross-pollination to take place. Elatum hybrid delphiniums are tetraploid with 32 chromosomes. The red species delphiniums are both diploid with 16.

The first successful hybridisation, between a red species and an elatum garden hybrid, was achieved at the Royal Moorheim Nursery, in Holland, by Dr. Theodore Ruys, who spent 30 years trying to produce a red delphinium of the elatum type. It was in 1929 that, quite by accident a purple hybrid appeared in a plantation of *D. nudicaule*. Further breeding involved selfing and back crossing of several generations of plants. Two selections of Ruysii type delphinium were made, 'Rose Queen' and 'Pink Sensation'. The latter remains in cultivation but is not a strong grower. It resembles a belladonna type delphinium, is sterile and may well be a triploid, having 24 chromosomes.

CHAPTER FIFTEEN

'Pink Lustre' seed became available, in 1938, in America from a plant of Charles Barber's 'Pearl Necklace' strain x *D. cardinale*. Plants are also recorded as growing in the garden of Mr. Burr Gregory, in Washington, in 1942 that were derived from *D. cardinale* x elatum hybrids. How these were obtained is not recorded but the assumption must be that they resulted from the discovery that colchicine treatment of the species would double the number of chromosomes and allow the resulting plants to be crossed with the garden hybrids. Use of colchicine, a toxic and carcinogenic chemical, by Dr. Gustav Mehlquist, a professor at the University of Connecticut, is well documented. His hybrids were derived from crossing the elatum garden hybrids with tetraploid *D. cardinale*.

Frank Reinelt, the raiser of the 'Giant Pacific' seed strains, wrote that his pink 'Astolat' series was obtained by irradiating seeds of *D. cardinale*. This induced chromosome doubling which produced a variety of mutated and distorted tetraploid seedlings, from which he bred an improved strain that was then crossed with the elatum hybrids. So far, where Britain is concerned, plants derived from this breeding work are the most garden-worthy and perennial of those that have red species in their ancestry. They are not, however, truly pink but are more accurately described as magenta in colouring.

Dr. Robert Legro, a Dutchman, started to investigate methods of crossing the red delphinium species with the elatum garden hybrids in 1953. It was in 1958, however, that he was successful, having crossed *D. nudicaule* and *D. cardinale* to produce a hybrid that was then treated with colchicine to double the chromosome count from 16 to 32. The resulting tetraploid hybrid was then crossed with an elatum hybrid cultivar described as 'Black and white', that came from 'Giant Pacific' stock to create a plant that was intermediate between the red species and an elatum garden hybrid, but with red, semi-double florets. From this first generation plant, successive generations were bred, either by crossing selected seedlings, or back-crossing on to elatum hybrids. Progress was good, with around 800 seedlings each year. These plants were grown at the Wageningen University, in Holland and therefore are called 'University Hybrids'.

Bob Legro's breeding programme was so promising that Blackmore and Langdon carried out a similar programme in the 1960's and early 1970's. Although they made good progress, the plants were found to suffer excessively from mildew and their constitution was considered suspect, so that the project was eventually abandoned.

Breeding in Holland, by Bob Legro, terminated when he retired in 1981 but the programme was transferred to the Royal Horticultural Gardens, at Wisley in Surrey. The plants were introduced, to the public, at the Chelsea flower show in 1986. The breeding work undertaken by Bob Legro is documented, in considerable detail, in a number of Delphinium Society Yearbooks.

Two relatively short growing 'University Hybrid' type delphiniums have been marketed in Britain, those being 'Princess Caroline', which is a clear pink, and 'Red Rocket' which is scarlet. Despite the tremendous amount of breeding work expended on these plants, they appear to lack perenniality, in Britain at least, which is undoubtedly due to the influence of the red delphinium species. It may be that they would be more successful in a different climate and, of course, large numbers are grown under glass, in Holland, for the cut flower trade.

ABOUT THE DELPHINIUM SOCIETY

By Les Cooper

The story of the Delphinium Society began in 1928 at a lunch held in the Grosvenor Hotel, London. Four men including Charles Langdon, who had founded the great delphinium nursery Blackmore and Langdon, and Tommy Carlile, a nurseryman who specialised in herbaceous plants, decided to call a meeting to see if there was sufficient general interest in a society dedicated to delphinium cultivation.

A meeting was held in September 1928 and it was decided to form the British Delphinium Society. The Secretary was to be Alec Moir, an amateur grower and the Chairman was Charles Langdon. The objectives of the new society were to encourage the production of new and improved varieties of delphiniums, to collect and disseminate information about delphiniums, to undertake trials, to organise and hold exhibitions and to publish an annual journal.

The first show was held on July 5th 1929 and it was a wonderful success. The R.H.S. New Hall was packed with delphiniums. However, most of the exhibits were from the trade with thirteen nurseries staging delphiniums while the amateur entries were sparse. At this time there were many nurseries supplying delphiniums for the many large estates and gardens that existed. Indeed although the B.D.S. took an "enlightened and sympathetic attitude towards the small amateur grower" it was quite trade oriented with forty-four professional growers listed as members in 1931. This tended to influence opinions and Year Book articles encouraged members to buy British delphiniums because foreign grown plants were inferior. There must have been a good number of wealthy members because special classes were included in the shows for the small man "who employs only a part-time gardener, or no gardener at all".

The first Year Book was published in 1930. The editor was S. Halford Roberts, a London dentist. The book was a very polished production with a small coloured photograph on the front and a nice full colour advertisement for Kelways of Langport in the centre. There were, also, greetings from the American Delphinium Society.

The British Delphinium Society continued to increase membership and produced more large shows. The emphasis was on quantity both in the garden and in the show hall. However, an amateur grower, Frank Bishop, began exhibiting large spikes that caused concern among some members who considered them coarse and rank. There was much discussion in the Year Books about the merits or demerits of large delphiniums.

Another point of contention was the existence of a Northern Delphinium Society. The B.D.S. claimed to be the national society and suggested that there should be a merger. The Northern Society held out and it wasn't until 1936 that the two became a true British Delphinium Society.

During the Second World War the ornamental side of horticulture in Great

Britain stood still as the "dig for victory" campaign persuaded gardeners to use their land for vegetable growing. Nevertheless, the B.D.S. continued to keep going, even publishing it's Year Book throughout.

In 1946 a show was held with five nurseries exhibiting as well as a reasonable number of entries from amateurs. At first membership increased but times had changed and finance was becoming a problem. There were no longer as many wealthy members with large gardens. In 1951 the annual show was cancelled because there was no trade support and few amateur entries due to a late season. The 1952 show was better but only Blackmore and Langdon gave support. Some members now felt that the B.D.S. had served its purpose and that it should become a hardy-plant society. In the Chairman's report for 1952 he suggested that a resolution to this effect should be passed at the Annual General Meeting. At this meeting there was a great deal of criticism and a new committee was appointed to look into the situation. At a resumed A.G.M on 20th January 1953 they proposed continuing as before. The old committee resigned and the new took over. Thus began a new era with two men leading the way; one was Reg Lucas who became Secretary while the other was Ronald Parrett who took over as Year Book editor.

Ronald Parrett worked as an accountant for Beaverbrook Newspapers and using a little Daily Express expertise he produced in 1954 a superb Year Book. In 1956 the American Delphinium Society ceased and the B.D.S. became The Delphinium Society. Membership then increased rapidly and Ronald Parrett became known as 'Mr Delphinium' appearing on television and writing a definitive book on delphiniums. Following the publication of the 1959 Year Book he gave up the editorship which he passed to George Cairncross. Meanwhile, the Secretary, Reg Lucas had been carefully working to get the Society on a sound financial footing. He was, also, a brilliant writer and eventually he became editor until his sad death in 1976.

The Delphinium Society had become a true amateur society, run by amateurs for amateurs. In 1978 the only surviving major delphinium nursery, Blackmore and Langdon decided to discontinue their breeding programme. The Society now realised that it had an important role to play; for many years now amateurs have introduced most of the new cultivars. Over the years Society members like Tom Cowan, Roy Latty, Duncan McGlashan, David and Shirley Basssett plus others too numerous to mention have been at the forefront of delphinium hybridising. Fortunately, there are now more sources of named delphiniums and hopefully they will become more and more popular.

The Delphinium Society is one of a number of specialist plant societies, run by dedicated enthusiasts, which perform an important and perhaps under-appreciated role in horticulture.

The Society provides a range of excellent benefits for its members, in return for a very modest annual subscription. Those include a colour illustrated Year Book, access to hand-pollinated and other seeds, the opportunity to participate in shows, cultivation classes and advice.

Membership enquiries should be addressed to:

The Delphinium Society,
2, The Grove, Ickenham,
Uxbridge, Middlesex,
UB10 8QH